Becoming Mad and Asking Why the River is Flowing

Allu Kuy

Copyright © 2014 by Allu Kuy
Cover art by Jef Cablog
All rights reserved.
No part of this publication may be reproduced, distributed, or transmitted in any form or by any means, including photocopying, recording, or other electronic or mechanical methods, without the prior written permission of the publisher, except in the case of brief quotations embodied in critical reviews and certain other noncommercial uses permitted by copyright law.

allukuy@gmail.com

ISBN: 1502955083
ISBN-13: 978-1-5029-5508-1

To the *invisibles*

♥ ♥ ♥

"Study me as much as you like,
you will not know me,
for I differ in a hundred ways from
what you see me to be.
Put yourself behind my eyes and
see me as I see myself,
for I have chosen to dwell in
a place you cannot see."

~ Rumi

The names of places and people in this book have been changed to protect their privacy.

CONTENTS

1. Being Lazy — 1
2. Hometown — 2
3. The Riddle — 4
4. The Great Flood — 10
5. The Big Ocean — 15
6. Magic and Miracles — 21
7. What Is Real? — 28
8. The Unbelievers — 38
9. The Kingdom of Heaven — 41
10. Freedom to Choose — 43
11. Clash of Worlds — 47
12. The Will of God — 58
13. A Secret — 69
14. The Haves and the Haves-Nots — 74
15. The Third World and the First World — 82
16. Dark Night of the Soul — 86
17. The Root of Evil — 91
18. A Young Urban Professional — 93
19. Fear of Death and Search for Love — 97
20. Confronting Fears — 100
21. It Is Only a Dream — 102
22. The Crow — 105
23. Freedom — 111

24. The Curse of God	113
25. Imagined Conversations	116
26. Why Is the River Flowing?	119
27. Redemption	121
28. The Nature of God	127
29. The Pre-Christian *Igorot* God	132
30. Soul Capture	137
31. To Find One's Self	139
32. Enlightenment	144
33. The Wicked Aunt	159
34. A Separate Journey	166
35. Insights from the Hallucination	169
36. Life After Death	173
37. On Earth, as It Is in Heaven	177
38. Glass Bubble Worlds	179
39. It Is Not Real	182
40. The Way Out of the Trap	184
41. The Will of Man	186
42. Only A Storytelling	189
43. The Great Storyteller	190
44. Closing Riddle	191
EPILOGUE	192

1

BEING LAZY

I was accused of being a sloth, the seventh deadly sin in Christian theology, after I quit my job and did nothing, as I could not come to terms with what God ordered in the Bible that I have to painfully toil the earth with the sweat of my brow in order to survive what I ironically found to be a pointless existence in a haphazard world. I was censured for being an unproductive member of society. And for defying God's rules and order, I was thought of as crazy.

My parents died the way they did because of their beliefs. They believed that to survive, we have to struggle hard by working very hard. They died of what I surmised was due to hard labor. I became cynical about their belief – the idea that in order to live, I must work hard for it, as if I have to pay a price for being born. Mother had told me that I was born to worship God and sing His praises. I did not want to believe her because God and His ways did not make sense to me. A scientist postulated that my birth was the result of the random impulses of nature, which could mean I am just an accident. The scientist also did not make sense. Time and again, I have wondered if my lazy, crazy existence is worth all the trouble of dragging myself through the hardships and uncertainties of life.

I had no problem giving in to what my 'accusers' thought of me. I relished my time doing nothing. I spent most of it in easy slumber. And in my sleep, I was entertained by many dreams. It was from these dreams that I was inspired to write a book, an endeavor which I had hoped would stop me from being a lazy, unproductive member of society. Although, perhaps, not from being crazy.

2

HOMETOWN

Cradled by tall, lush, and rugged mountains, my hometown lies within the interior regions of the Cordillera Central on the island of Luzon, Philippines. It is a small, self-sufficient, subsistence rice farming village-town. The mountains were carved into stonewalled rice terraces and vegetable gardens. While some parts of the forests are cleared for swidden farming, most of the forest cover remains intact as they are being used as hunting grounds and as a sustainable source of wood and wild herbs for the villagers.

Root crops, rice, and vegetables were traditionally the primary foods, supplemented by meat from forest animals, fish, frogs, and crabs from streams and rivers. Swine and fowl were customarily sacrificed for ceremonial purposes only and were not raised for home consumption. However, as the practice of hunting has declined in recent generations, meat from livestock has become a more common source of household food.

The town is a cluster of several small settlements. At the center of the town is a valley of rice fields. A vibrantly flowing river cuts through this valley. Some of the villagers' dwellings are nestled in small patches of low, gentle slopes along the river next to rice fields, while others are perched high up on mountain ridges. On ordinary days, the village-town is very quiet, except for the occasional squeal of pigs, barking of dogs, and chatter of chickens. The only sound heard day and night, without interruption, is the murmur of the river, whose sound is only temporarily drowned out during the season of festivities when the cool and crisp mountain air reverberates with the beat of sonorous gongs.

I am the youngest of the dozen children of my parents. My

mother, like her mother and grandmothers before her, worked daily in the fields. This was how we got our staples like root crops, rice, and vegetables. My father, on the other hand, deviated from the traditional occupations of his forefathers. He did not become a hunter or a full-time farmer. He was a civil servant. His salary provided us with cash to buy necessities that we could not easily produce on our own, such as salt, sugar, soap, school supplies, and clothing.

In the days of my childhood, nature readily provided the most basic needs, and needs that went beyond the basic were the concern of parents and other grown-ups. The lush forests, verdant hills, clear streams, and rivers were the village children's familiar playground. The air and water are fresh and clean. Village children, wild and free, ran, jumped, climbed trees, mountains and boulders, and collected wild berries to snack on. Totally oblivious of the wilder world that I would soon come to know as I grew up, like most children, I lived in my little natural, magical bubble world in that little dreamy village-town.

3

THE RIDDLE

When I was very young and not yet in school, it was mainly my mother's mother, my very old grandmother, who looked after me and started my early education. Grandma lived in a hut on top of a mountain, which was occasionally shrouded by huge passing clouds and mists in the early morning and late afternoon. As a child, I disliked going to her house due to its distance and high elevation. To get to her hut, I had to climb a steep footpath which, in a child's physical smallness and relative perception, appeared to be very far away. Grandma, however, had been very generous to come to my parents' house to babysit me while my parents were away at work. Mother usually left for work before the sun peeked over the eastern mountains, and she came back home when the sun had already sunk behind the hills. Father was also often out of town because of his work.

Reflecting on it many years later, I could only imagine Grandma: a small, very old, stooping woman, supported by a walking stick, with big toes deformed and the soles of her feet as hard as thick leather, having not worn any footwear since the day she was born. She descends from her mountain top, traverses the valley of rice fields, then climbs another mountain top to where my family house is located. It must have been an arduous trek for a very old, stooping woman to make that return trip almost every day.

Grandma had always struck me as a puzzling figure. I remember her well, with her tousled hair, toothless grin, and eyes disappearing into slits when she laughed. It is still very vivid in my memory, one very cold but bright and sunny morning, as Grandma and I sat in the front yard of my parents' house for our daily routine of sunning ourselves. Sitting on a low wooden bench, Grandma was quietly smoking her pipe. Her thoughtful gaze was fixed on the horizon before us. I was sitting on the stone steps, contentedly watching and counting a group of about five or six boys walking one after the other down a narrow foot trail on the opposite hillside across the river. Grandma remarked that she thought they were heading downstream to catch some fish. My pet cat sat quietly by my side, eyes tightly shut, drowsing in the early morning sun. A couple of month-old puppies, just having been suckled, snugly rested on their mother's belly. It was all a very quiet and peaceful scenario.

At the edge of the stonewalled paddies, just above the riverbank, we could see a number of villagers on their way to work in the fields. They appeared tiny against the backdrop of mountain walls, the golden valley of ripening rice plants, and the glistening serpentine river in the middle. Most of the women were carrying large squarish woven baskets perfectly balanced on top of their heads. Their hips swayed as they walked on the very narrow edges of the rice terraces. The men were carrying woven rattan backpacks that hung from their broad shoulders. I was quietly watching this extremely ordinary, everyday, scenario, when it occurred to me to ask Grandma about something which had been intriguing me. I have been wondering where the river is coming from and where it is going to – where it begins and where it ends. So, I asked Grandma those questions.

She gave me a surprised look, as if she was also thinking about the river, or the people, or the mountains, and that I had coincidentally tuned into her contemplative mood.

"Forti-forti-yah.
Adi kaila nan ikor ko; adi kaila nan urok.
Ay into pay nan narpoak? Ay into pay nan umayak?[1]

---

[1] Literally, Where am I coming from, where am I going to?

... Hinu ak pay?"

"A riddle, a riddle.
You cannot see my tail; you cannot see my head.
Where do I begin? Where do I end?"
... Who Am I?"

"The river!"

I pointed, excitedly, to the river. I just knew that the answer to Grandma's riddle must be the river. The image that occurred in my mind as she uttered her riddle was that of a snake – a snake whose head and tail were not visible – just like the river slithering in my hometown!

Grandma mysteriously smiled, as if she was pleased with my answer. She did not say anything. After one or two more leisurely puffs on her tapering smoke pipe, she carefully emptied the pipe by gently tapping it upside down on a piece of log. She let go of one deep breath and beckoned,

"Come sit by my side, *Apu*[2] . I will tell you the Story of the River."

"The water in the river comes down from the sky," Grandma began her tale about what she claimed was the river's origin.

"The mountains you see around you are bridges for the water to descend from the sky to earth. The water flows down the

---

[2] Apu is a term of respect. In English, it connotes the meaning of master, leader, or divine. It is a term that is used interchangeably to refer to both a grandparent and a grandchild. A grandparent refers to his grandchild as apu, and a grandchild refers to his grandparent as apu. Villagers also use it to respectfully announce their presence when visiting another villager's home. In this context, when a caller says apu, the latter is drawing the attention of the house's occupants. Apu can also mean leader when used as a prefix to the name of a leader, such as the town priest, the president of the country, the elders, and all other kinds of leaders. In modern times, God is also referred to as Apu, as in Apu Dios and Apu Hesus. And, similar to the phrase 'Oh my God! The villagers would say 'ay Apu!' to express surprise, disappointment, and so on.

mountains through streams and waterfalls, and through the mud channels our ancestors furrowed to irrigate our rice fields. Some of the water remains to form lakes and springs in the forests, and this is for the forest dwellers to drink and bathe themselves. On its way down, it passes through all the different settlements, providing each and every household with clean and fresh water to drink. The rest of it flows to the bottom of the mountains, forming what we now call a river. Now, the river is a nice home to fishes, frogs, and crabs, which we catch, and so we have some tasty fish, frogs and crabs to eat, sometimes." She glanced at me, smiling.

"So why don't you eat frogs and eels when we have them?"

"I don't eat those and certain other foods because there are things that a strange old woman like me should not eat," she said, and laughed.

"Why, Apu? Is it because you do not like how they taste?"

"No. It is because my father told me that if I am going to doctor people like he and his mother did, I should also not eat those foods."

"Are you a doctor, Apu?" I said, peeking at her, slightly amused.

"A retired one," she announced proudly, then giggled.

I thought her joke was really funny, so I laughed. She stared at me, a thin smile forming on her lips. She scratched her head and started to laugh. She appeared to be amused by me, laughing at her. I laughed at her because she was, again, being funny, claiming to be a doctor, and a retired one at that! We were like one very old woman and one very young girl, laughing for no reason at all. When our silliness subsided, I again turned to the river.

"Where does the river go, Apu?"

"The journey of the river is long and arduous," Grandma spoke, shifting into a serious tone. "It flows downstream, passing through obstacles and blockages. The river visits many more villages, towns, and even big cities on its long journey. It may become dirty and poisoned along the way, but the river continues to flow in accordance with its nature."

"Look at that stretch of the river over there." Grandma pointed at a downturn bend in the river where boulders and a big fallen tree blocked the river's path. "Down there, the river is rough, turbulent, but very lively, is it not?" she asked as she calmly glanced at me. "Compare it to the quiet, smooth flowing river over there." She pointed at another part of the same river by jutting out her chin.

I looked at both places she pointed to. I told her what Mother and Father thought about that turbulent part of the river. They thought it was extremely dangerous and could kill, and so they always scolded my two elder brothers, who were always excited about riding an inflatable rubber tube on that part of the river.

Grandma nodded knowingly, and said something about the river being like people. She explained that the boys loved the thrill of riding a rubber tube because, as they rode the current and felt the might of the water as it overcame obstacles, they shared in the excitement as they triumphed over turbulence. She said that the tension and action the boys had to exert to navigate their way through the rapids strengthened their muscles and built their confidence, so it was good for them.

In a very thoughtful, almost dreamy tone, Grandma compared the parallel between the river's natural flow and a human being's life. She said that just like the river's flow, life is naturally sometimes smooth and sometimes rough, and that a rough flow is good as it stirs or shakes the life within each one of us, through which we are either inspired or compelled to swim to make it through. Grandma said that it is when the river stops flowing and becomes still and stagnant in one place that it meets its death.

We were suddenly distracted by the shrill cry of a baby chicken. Apparently, it was lost, for we could see the mother hen and the rest of the brood a few meters away, blithely pecking in between the glazed stones paving the front yard. I went to investigate. I found that one of the chicks fell into a narrow canal. The chick was very confused and afraid. I thought how amazing it was that, in contrast to its physical smallness and softness, such a fragile, tiny bird could let out a very sharp, determined and annoying cry for its mother. On impulse, I picked it up with the intention of putting it near the rest of the brood. As I picked it up and held it in my small hand, however, it squawked even louder, alerting the mother hen, who came running and cackling. At about three feet away, the hen abruptly paused, hunched, and threatened to attack me. Surprised and intimidated, I dropped the chick, which quickly ran towards its mother. The hen extended her wings to secure the chick. They were joined by the other raucous chicks that came running after the mother hen. After a little while, when she felt it safe, the mother hen gradually relaxed her ruffled feathers.

I walked back towards Grandma. She chuckled as she peeked at me, as if there was something very funny about the incident.

"Their mother is a scary monster," I said bluntly.

"The little chick got lost and it panicked," Grandma said as I sat down.

Then she mentioned something about the baby chicken's predicament, which she likened to a person being lost. I was surprised when she said that, like that chick which fell into the ditch, even I, could get lost – that I may find myself alone in strange, dark, and scary corners of the world, calling for my mother, and that, wherever she might be, Mother would come for me, if I believed she would. Grandma's strange words did not make sense to me at that time, but that did not bother me as everyone else in the family was used to her not making sense most of the time. Grandma, herself, was a riddle to me.

4

THE GREAT FLOOD

One chilly and stormy night, as the wind howled and lashed outside, Grandma and I were safely cooped up inside, warming ourselves in front of the kitchen hearth. I heard that a powerful typhoon was passing through. Despite the stormy weather, Mother went to her Catholic Women's League meeting, and Father, I was told, was traveling to the next town to attend a very important meeting. Grandma was asked to spend the night at our house. After dinner, my two immediate elder brothers went to their room, probably doing their school homework or already sleeping. Evenings were usually cold in the mountains, and having no electric power, we went to bed as early as it got dark.

Grandma and I sat side by side, sipping mountain tea leaves. A pot of broth was simmering over the fire. Grandma said that we were going to thoroughly stew the broth of red beans and a piece of deer meat to make them tender, ready to be reheated for breakfast the next morning. Without any preliminaries, she resumed her tale about the river:

"Last summer, when we went to the distant field upstream, we stopped to drink and rest by a creek. Do you remember that creek?" she asked.

"Yes," I replied as the image of that particular creek flashed in my mind.

"You saw that that little river had very little water. Many creeks in the upstream fields have been like that in recent years, and it is worrying me a little." She spoke in a low, thoughtful voice.

"As the mountain streams dry up, the rivers will soon follow. But they are not actually dying, they are just going underground. A time will come when they will suddenly resurface with great force that will frighten the life out of us." She now spoke strongly with a trace of excitement in her voice.

Puzzled, I slowly turned my head to look at her. She did not seem to care about my perplexed reaction. My eyes followed her movement as she quietly raised her cup to her mouth. She sipped her tea, slowly but noisily. Her pensive gaze was fixed on the crackling fire in front of us. She gave me the impression that she was thinking aloud to herself more than talking to me. Without minding me, she continued talking:

"Rivers may become so weak that they appear to die if we cut down all the trees in the mountains. During the dry season, the waterways will be dehydrated, and our rice paddies will harden and crack. We will then have to seek water from the next town, but if they don't have enough water because they've cut down all their trees and sold them by the truckload, they will disagree with us. Then we either do something else to get water, or we battle with them."

I glanced up at her, bewildered by the words she spoke. Although my rational mind could not fully comprehend what she was saying, it seemed that my young body felt what she meant as I found myself tensely sitting upright on my chair. Then I had an idea about what she might be referring to: I had recently overheard Mother and Father discussing a dispute with our neighboring town upstream. Father had been attending a meeting where they were discussing a dispute with the upstream people whom my townspeople accused of cutting down many of our trees and making big profits by selling them to buyers from a bigger town. The upstream people, on the other hand, are claiming that the trees are within their 'legal' territory. To travel to the bigger town, which is the capital of our province, we have to pass by the territory of the upstream people, and they have been threatening to block off our passage and isolate us if we insist on our claim. This incident stirred rumors of an impending tribal war between my townspeople and the upstream people.

Grandma continued talking:

"And when the rain comes, there will be a flood of water rushing down the bald mountains. The millions of stones, hauled by our ancestors to build the stonewalled rice terraces, will crumble on us, maiming and killing us! The river will rise and flood our farms and villages, drowning our pigs, chickens, dogs, and us, just as it did long, long ago, during the time of our great- great-grandparents."

The wind had stopped howling outside. A long silence transpired. The flame's flickering light and soft crackling sound intermittently interrupted the still darkness surrounding me and Grandma. In my mind, her ominous words formed a vivid image of a dangerous, angry river. I suddenly felt afraid. Through the corner of my eye, I could see Grandma's intense, yet deeply placid gaze, steadily focused on the flickering flame. She leaned forward to adjust the firewood. She blew air into the dying fire. Tiny sparks jumped up and down and the fire blazed. She turned to look at me. She smiled kindly with a playful twinkle in her eyes.

She shifted her gaze back towards the fire, and, for what seemed to be an endless moment, none of us said anything.

I broke the seemingly timeless silence when I spoke, "Please tell me that story of the flood a long time ago. Did it drown even cats?"

I glanced at the cat, sitting in complete stillness, gazing at the flames, as if entranced by it.

"It was a very long, long time ago, according to the story I heard from my own grandma, when our villages were sitting on flat land, and not on mountains as they are now. They said that it was better at that time because nobody could get lost in the forest. It was easier to hunt, and there were many animals roaming our forests. The men hunted, and the women went with them if they so wished. There was a belief back then that when a man's wife was pregnant, the man should not go traveling or hunting. But there was this one man who did not observe the beliefs and customs. When all the other villagers had left for their fields, he took his hunting gear and set off towards the forest. He had not gone very far when his pregnant wife came running after him, saying, 'Wait for me. Let's go together'. Upon hearing his wife's call, instead of slowing down, he quickened his pace so that his wife could not catch up with him. *Kafunyan*[3] saw what was happening. Kafunyan said he would dam the rivers and flood the town to create mountains to hinder and prevent men with pregnant wives from hunting. The sky darkened, and for one day and one night, heavy rain poured down, relentlessly. The rivers quickly rose and submerged everything in sight. It was said that only the tip of our highest mountain was visible. There was a brother and a sister who were able to run to the mountain's peak. After many days, when the water was receding, the siblings were in for a big surprise – lo and behold! Everything changed! The flat lands became these bumpy mountains!" Grandma giggled with a comical look on her face, as if what happened a long time ago was a magical fairy tale.

"And then?" I asked.

"It was said that while the brother and sister were taking refuge on the peak of the highest mountain, they shivered with cold and hunger. And then, they saw smoke rising from another distant mountain peak! They asked a wild cat to swim to the opposite peak to get and bring back fire. The cat went on the mission, but it did not come back. After a couple more days, they asked another wild cat to go to the opposite mountain to get and bring back fire. The cat set out, and they waited for it to return. And then, one day, just

---

[3] God or deity.

as they were about to lose hope, they saw, from across the opposite direction, a star-like object. As they looked on, the object became bigger and brighter. Then they realized it was heading straight for them! How distressed they were indeed! They thought it was coming to finish them off.

When the star-like object came near enough to be identified, they were relieved and delighted to see that it was the second cat they had sent off. The cat, swimming, held a blazing pine torch in its mouth. It arrived and passed the fire on to them."

Grandma paused as she roared a big yawn. She looked at me in a way as if to say that that was the end of the story. I begged her to tell me more. She yawned again, softly rubbing my back, saying that if she told me more, it would take us until morning.

5

THE BIG OCEAN

There was a clearing in the forest where there was an *ugwor*[4]. Often, when it was sunny, Grandma took me there. The source of the water, according to her, was very deep, coming from deep beneath the earth. This particular ugwor has never run out of water, even during the driest summers when other springs and streams would have dried up. Grandma told me that very long ago, when I and even my parents were not yet born and when most of our town was still an uncleared jungle, this particular spot was the favorite of birds and wild animals that came to drink, bathe, and rest.

In the long days of summer, Grandma and I hung out at the ugwor in the forest, and with my imagination, I never tired of playing with the little wildflowers, rocks, twigs, pinecones, and even tiny beetles. Meanwhile, if she was not telling me stories, Grandma sat under a huge, ancient tree. She would leisurely smoke her pipe as she watched me play. I could get so engrossed in my playing, but at occasional intervals, I checked on her. I sometimes caught a glimpse of her with her eyes closed, leaning her back against the tree. I believed she was drowsing, although it always amazed me how she managed to remain sitting upright while napping. There were times I thought I heard her saying something to me. I looked at her only to see her lips moving, but her eyes remained closed.

One time, while I was filling up with water the little holes and ditches, I furrowed at the edge of the ugwor, a question popped up in my mind:

---

[4] Spring water

"Why does the river keep flowing, Apu? Where is the river's water going?" I called out loud to her so she could hear me.

"Come over here," she called back.

I stood up, rubbed the dirt off my hands and walked towards the huge, old tree.

She tapped her walking stick on a fat protruding tree root to her right, motioning for me to sit.

"It is the nature of a river to flow. It has a purpose."

"What purpose?" I asked.

Grandma hesitated for a moment. She appeared to be eager to make me understand what she meant, and what she was about to say, but she seemed to be having a hard time finding the right words in order for me to understand.

"It keeps on flowing because it is its nature to go to its destination."

"Where is the destination?"

"All rivers travel and furrow their own unique trails to go downstream. Rivers of all sizes, colors, and characters meld and become one in the *big ocean*."

"What is the big ocean, Apu? How does it look like?"

Grandma laughed at my question. Then she said that the big ocean is an immensely huge river whose dimensions extend forever. She said that in its immensity, I may not be able to imagine it, not unless, maybe, I have a glimpse of it myself. Grandma's old eyes sparkled. A thin smile formed on her lips as she gazed at me.

I tried to imagine the big ocean, but it was impossible for me to picture an enormously large river whose dimensions extended forever. The river in my hometown is quite small compared to the big river in the provincial capital, which I saw when Father brought me along on one of his travels. I just could not imagine a much more massive river whose length seemed to go on forever. I cast a sidelong glance at Grandma. I wondered if she was telling me a *real story*.

After a brief silence, more tobacco puffs and a coarse cough, Grandma, who had been observing me, picked up her walking stick and gently tapped the ground a few times as she gleefully chuckled.

Abruptly, I stood up and ran back to my play. The sun was shining, and the forest seemed to respond by reflecting back the luminosity. Moved by a gentle wind, the trees produced a cool breeze. The water in the pond quivered and sparkled. My attention was caught by a couple of blue butterflies that playfully fluttered about. I got up and chased them, but I tripped over a tree root fully covered with glowing yellow-green lichens. Before me, on a long, shimmering green leaf, sat a striking black-dotted orange ladybug. It was an ordinary ladybug, but, at that moment, it was the most stunning bug I had ever seen. I only slightly touched it with my index finger when it dropped itself on the soft carpet of green lichens, and then it gathered itself up and flew away. I noticed the crawling plants with oddly shaped leaves; their round, tiny, and shiny deep red fruits dotted the forest floor. At that moment, I felt as if the colors around me intensified and vibrated. The forest was a sheer wonderland. Fascinated, I turned to look at Grandma. She was also looking at me.

♥ ♥ ♥

Many years later, after her death, I learned that Grandma

never had the chance to travel outside our remote village-town. In her days, traveling was neither easy nor practical. There were no roads and no transports. Depending on how far one wanted to travel, one would have to walk for several days across many mountains and rivers to reach the next village or town. So I do not know where she got the idea about the big ocean. She had never been near the sea. I deduced that, perhaps, she had heard it from the stories of the few villagers who wandered to the lowland towns and came back with interesting stories about the sea and the flat lowland places they had seen. If I knew back then that she had never seen the ocean, I certainly would have asked how she knew about it. Although she had never seen the ocean, she believed that there is a huge, unending river where rivers of all colors, sizes, and characters flow to.

I was nine years old when Grandma stopped coming to my house. She became too old to continue the trek all the way from her hilltop abode. The following year, a few days after my 10th birthday, she passed away. People say she died of old age. Although people spoke of her as being the oldest person in town at the time of her death, nobody really knows how old she was. When she was still alive, I once asked her how old she was. She replied that she did not count her age because counting one's age made one get old faster than necessary. My grade school teacher was very curious; she asked me how old my grandma was when she died. I did not know, so I asked Mother. Mother's answer was that when Grandma was born, they did not have a calendar on their wall, so no one knows exactly when Grandma was born.

I could not understand why nobody knew when Grandma was born. I have memorized the birth dates of my immediate two elder brothers, as well as the birth dates of my cousins and playmates who are around the same age as me. Mother explained that at that time of her death, Grandma was the oldest person in town, so as no one was older than her, and no one alive was born in the same period that she was born in, no one could claim to know her birth date. Mother further explained that in Grandma's time, they did not count the years and months like we do. They did not consult a paper calendar to determine the passage of time. They also did not have clocks and watches. Instead, they calculated time by observing the changing faces of the moon as it appeared at night and the position of the sun as they saw it during the daytime. Mother said that the old way of ascertaining time was known to all village folks by heart. They knew when to do a particular task in the fields, when to perform a certain ritual, when to plant a particular crop, when certain bird species visited, when the typhoons came, when to have festivities, and when to proclaim communal or public holidays. They did not adhere to a fixed weekly, monthly, or yearly holiday schedule as we currently do. People were free to take a day off from work whenever they felt the need for it. And when the old people deemed it necessary, based on certain age-old traditional auspices and guidance, special public holidays were announced.

It turned out that in Grandma's time, *time* did not control or dictate their activities. Instead, they performed their activities anytime, as they saw it appropriate for their well-being.

♥ ♥ ♥

As a storyteller, Grandma was certainly enthralling that when I was absorbed listening to her stories, I felt as if I were seeing a full-fledged movie in front of me. Some of her stories I liked the best include the following: the hunter who married a female spirit of the forest; the gigantic reptile that devoured villagers; The Great Flood; the man from the sky who appeared after the Great Flood – he went from village to village to distribute animals, plant seeds, and he taught people some useful crafts; the seven celestial sisters who descended to swim and play in a forest lake when the moon was full; the feared beings who roamed at night to steal snoring people's consciousness by nibbling at their flesh; the hunter who was engulfed by a quickmud, thereby discovering the existence of a subterranean village, and; the tale of the very old, teeny-weeny woman who lived in a teeny-weeny hut and who had a magic ladle that cooked something out of nothing. Meanwhile, a handful of Grandma's tales such as the above Story of the River, the story of The Laughing Trees, the Still Water of River Kok, and, the Mourning Owl, were stories I found intimidating and difficult to fully comprehend.

Another entertaining story Grandma used to tell were her *dreams* – they were stories she saw while she slept.

6

MAGIC AND MIRACLES

My mother, just like her mother, was a competent storyteller. Many nights, if she was not too tired from working in the fields, she would tell my two older brothers and me stories. Sainoc is three years older than me, while Samier is five years older. There was one time when Sainoc and I were discussing whose tales we liked better – whether it was Grandma's or Mother's. It was difficult to decide as all their stories were engaging. But, over time, I came to prefer Mother's real stories about a very intriguing, old, white bearded God and His Crucified Son. Mother's stories, I was told, were about real people, real events, real battles, and real miracles. I became convinced that Mother's tales were indeed more real than Grandma's because they even taught them in school. In third grade, I was awarded the 'best in religion' medal at the end of the school year for being the most knowledgeable about Bible stories. At the Baptist Church's summer bible school, where my friend Mercy and I attended, while Mercy was bestowed the 'most behaved" accolade, I received the 'best in memory verse'. In addition, during our graduation from the month-long Summer Bible School, all of us children who had consistent attendance were given presents of candies, cookies, and praise for how smart and well-behaved we had been during the program. To add to its credibility, Mother's tales were recorded in the Bible book, which the foreign town priest sometimes read from when he delivered his Sunday speeches. Eventually, Sainoc and I agreed that Mother's stories were the real deal, as even strangers from far away foreign lands took the trouble to travel all the way to our village-town to show us movies about God, and His Crucified Son. When I asked Mother about these strangers, she told me that these kind and generous people came to spread the Gospel of God to all the corners of the world, including our little corner of the world. In comparison, Sainoc and I somewhat suspected that some of Grandma's stories, such as the traveling river, the laughing trees, and the mourning owl, were just improvised tales she concocted in her mind.

Grandma's stories were full of magic. Mother's stories were full of miracles. When I asked what the difference was between magic and miracle, Mother explained that magic is the work of the Devil, whereas miracle is the work of God.

Mother was a devout Catholic. She was a very active member of the local Catholic Women's League. She unfailingly went to Mass every Sunday, and she always had me in tow. It was impressed upon my young mind that going to church on Sundays was an absolute duty. In the catechism class in school, it was compulsory to memorize the Ten Commandments of God, and one of those commands was to honor and make holy the Sabbath day. The catechist had a complicated explanation (which up to this day, I still could not understand) when he stressed that breaking one of the Ten Commandments meant breaking them all. So, on the very rare occasions when Mother and I were unable to attend Mass, she felt very guilty, believing that we were committing sin by failing to obey the command of God to honor the 'Sabbath day'. And as Mother felt bad and guilty about herself, I also felt bad and guilty about myself.

One Sunday, on our way home from attending Mass, I asked Mother, "Where did God come from?"

"God exists all the time," she replied after some thought.

Not satisfied with her abstruse answer, I asked again, "But where did God come from?"

Mother silently pondered my question as we slowly trudged up the long stone steps leading to our house. I kept quiet and waited. Finally, she said, "It's not easy to explain. Ask your father."

♥ ♥ ♥

"Dad, where did God come from?"

Father furrowed his thick brows, confounded by the unexpected question. After some thinking, he referred me back to Mother.

"Ask your mother. She's the one who is always reading that thick and heavy book."

Mother's Bible was huge and heavy, with many colorful pictures. As it was the only colorful book in the house, I flipped through the pages with the pictures, over and over without getting bored. Mother treasured her Holy Bible the same way she treasured the family photos. And just like in the family photos, we little children were not allowed to touch the Bible without properly washing and drying our hands first.

♥ ♥ ♥

"Ma, why does God live in heaven in the sky?"

"God does not live in heaven. He is right beside you. He is everywhere. You know the song, 'Yahweh I know you are near', don't you?"

Mother's answer confused me because somebody once told me that God lives up high in heaven, above the clouds while Lucifer lives in hell, deep down, under the earth. Her back turned as she washed the dishes, Mother started singing and humming:

"Yahweh I know you are near,

> standing always at my side.
> Hmmm . . . hmmm . . ."

"If God is right beside me, if He is everywhere, why can't I see Him?" I interrupted her.

"Because He is a spirit. You cannot see a spirit."

I was squatting on the floor, one hand inattentively petting the cat, which was lying on its back. The cat playfully tried to claw my hand while I pondered about God as a spirit. Mother continued her melodious humming.

"Ma."

"What?"

"Why did God make angels and us?"

"God created the angels, and us, people, so we serve and worship Him, sing praises to Him, and pray to Him, just like we do in church," Mother explained.

"Why does God wants us to serve and worship Him, sing praises and pray to Him?"

"So we make Him happy."

"Is God unhappy?"

Silence. Mother knew that I was waiting for her answer. She cleared her throat noisily. She scratched her head lightly as she turned to face me. "You'll have to wait," she said, looking me in the eyes, "I'll ask Father Norberto about this".

I believe Mother never asked our town priest, Father Norberto, for she never got back to me with the answer.

♥ ♥ ♥

One evening, we listened, wide-eyed, as Mother related the incredible story of Samson, the superman of the Bible. According to the tale of Samson, with just his bare hands, he tore a lion's mouth apart and killed the beast.

"Ma, is Samson stronger than a lion?" I interrupted the storytelling.

"God gave Samson *special strength*, because God wanted him to lead the people of Israel."

"Why did Samson's parents disapprove of the beautiful girl that Samson liked?"

"Because she was a Philistine."

"What is a Philistine?"

"A Philistine is a Gentile. And Samson's parents did not want him to marry her because Gentiles are pagans."

"What is a Gentile? What is a pagan?"

"A Gentile is anybody who is not an Israelite. A pagan is somebody who does not believe in God, but worships other gods and not the one true God. Gentiles and pagans are *Unbelievers*."

"What is Israelite?"

At this point, the storytelling was getting so delayed that Sainoc was growing impatient.

"Shut-up, you are asking too many questions!" he bawled as he elbowed my ribs.

"Israelites are the people of Israel. They are *Believers*, and they are the Chosen People of God."

"Chosen People of God?"

"Yes," Mother said, curtly.

♥ ♥ ♥

Another evening, Mother, my two brothers, and I went to a free admission movie in the town square. At that time, there was neither electricity nor television in town, but occasionally, using a gasoline generator, some foreigners came to show movies to the villagers. The movies consisted mostly of Bible stories and, on occasion, the lives of white Christian families. If a Bible story was being shown, the dialogues were usually dubbed into our local language so villagers could understand the story. These movies were certainly bedazzling; they transported little children like me to other worlds.

The church basement, where the movie was to be shown, was fully packed. On this certain evening, the movie was about a great flood where Noah, his wife and children, collected a pair of each of the different kinds of animals and put them in a massive boat that Noah built. Noah was mandated by God to do this because, apart from him and his family, whose hearts were pure, all the other people were sinners, and so they were condemned by God to be punished by flooding.

"Ma!" I yelled, clutching her sleeves, just when the raging water was rising, destroying and submerging all the people, animals, and mountains. "Shh," Mother glared at me while an embarrassed Samier pinched me hard on the side.

After the movie, I could no longer hold my excitement; as soon as we exited the church basement, I blurted out to Mother:

"So Apu's story was true after all! A great flood submerged our villages! Animals and people died, except for a brother and sister who climbed the highest mountain in our town!"

Mother ignored what I said.

"So it was not only Noah and his family who survived the flood then?" I asked, glancing up at Mother, eager for an answer.

Mother winced, her face turned serious, as if suddenly lost in deep thoughts. She did not say anything.

As we got home, my two brothers and I could not stop babbling about the dramatic movie we had just seen. My big sister, who was home from college, burst out laughing, teasing and telling us that movies are *not real*, and that we were being silly and gullible for believing in them!

Grandma's stories, according to my friend Mercy's father, were only rumors. He said that they might in fact all be lies, because nobody had actually seen if the characters and events in the stories were real. Mercy's mother and my big brother, Tomas, both confirmed that Grandma's tales were not real. They all agreed that her tales were merely stories from long ago that old people told to gather little children, amuse them, or keep them quiet if they were being noisy or disorderly.

To learn that Grandma's tales were, after all, not real, disconcerted me. But if the movie was not real and yet Grandma, who had never seen a movie nor read a book, tells a story similar to the movie, *what is real then?* How do we know which stories are real?

7

WHAT IS REAL?

"Ma, I have seen the Holy Ghost again."

"What are you talking about?" Mother scowled as she turned to look at me.

I related to her the amorphous thing I had sometimes seen while lying in bed, awake, in the daytime, as I absentmindedly stared at the wall in front of me.

"Hush, it's just your overactive imagination again. Don't be thinking too much. It is *not real*, OK?" Mother, obviously, was not pleased.

"But I was not thinking! I was only staring at the wall." I responded, very sure of what I saw.

"How do you know it was not the Devil that you saw?" Samier, who had been listening, asked.

"I know because it smiled at me, and it did not have horns on its head," I responded, animatedly.

Mother again sternly stressed that what I saw was not real, and that I should not insist, nor even talk about it.

"Silly little one," Samier teased as he widened his eyes and stuck his tongue out.

♥ ♥ ♥

The next time Grandma came over to my house, I told her about the Holy Ghost. She was puzzled at first.

"What is a hu-lee goose?" she inquired.

Grandma, whose tongue was not accustomed to English words pronounced it as 'hu-lee gus', so I slowly guided her to say it as 'ho-lee gos'. She giggled as she tried to pronounce it as I did. I explained to her that the Holy Ghost, according to Mother, is a ghost sent by God.

It was not my first time seeing the "Holy Ghost". But it was only after I learned about the Christian concept of the Holy Ghost from Mother that I learned a word to articulate that thing I sometimes saw when I stared blankly at the wall.

I related to Grandma how I was lying on the bed, staring at the wall in front of me, for I did not know how long, when I saw it. I described to her how it gazed down at me in a very odd way, and as I looked on, sometimes it was there, sometimes not. Then Grandma started laughing. She laughed so hard that tears came rolling down her wrinkled cheeks. I became embarrassed and self-conscious, thinking that perhaps even Grandma now thinks I have turned into a fool. She stopped laughing to catch her breath as she wiped her tears with the back of her hand. Smiling a toothless grin, she tenderly looked down at me. Her moist eyes twinkled.

"Is it real, Apu?"

"Of course it's real," she coughed between more chuckles.

I did not expect her affirmative answer. Although I somehow felt reassured by her confirmation, I thought she was just pulling my leg.

"How does the hu-lee gus look like?" she asked, showing amused interest.

I tried to find words to describe the "Holy Ghost" but words eluded me. Sensing my difficulty, she encouraged me:

"Does it look like a human being?"

"I'm not sure . . . . Its eyes look at me, smiling."

"Animal?"

"I don't know," I said, shaking my head.

"Male or female?"

I shrugged my shoulders.

"Did you feel afraid?"

"No, I didn't."

Then she fell strangely quiet. Her deep, contemplative gaze, looking very far away.

"Is it really real?" I wanted to double-check.

"It is real," she reassured, glancing at me with a gentle smile.

"If it's really, really *real*, then how come Mother couldn't see it even though we sleep in the same room?" I asked.

"Because she *doesn't want* to see it."

"Is it a spirit?" I asked.

"Yes. It is a spirit."

"Mother said we cannot see spirits."

"Why not? I see them every day."

♥ ♥ ♥

I went to see Grandma at her hilltop abode to deliver some goods. It was a mild afternoon. We sat on some dry grass outside her hut. From our vantage point on that high place, we had a very good view over most part of the town's landscape.

"Are your stories real?" I asked the question I had long been wanting to ask her.

She stared at me for a couple of moments. She seemed to wonder what I meant by the question. She did not say anything but kept herself busy gathering spilled tobacco leaves and putting them back into an old wrinkled plastic bag.

"The giant snake with legs that hid in the river and devoured children, is it a true story?" I asked, suspiciously eyeing her.

She remained quiet.

"Apu, are you telling the truth? You're not lying, are you," I demanded.

She still did not say anything.

Annoyed by her prolonged silence and nonchalance, I pointed at her and said, "Liars go to hell; you're going to go to hell, Apu!" I bluntly told her what the priest in church had told me about lying and liars.

She remained quiet but composed. She seemed to be considering what to say to me. I continued eyeing her with a skeptical look and an impish grin.

"The *tabfiad*[5] did not eat only children, but grownups too; that's why our great-great-grandparents had to pack up and move to different other places," she spoke thoughtfully

The story of the tabfiad, or giant snake, is one of the more intriguing folktales in my hometown. Some people today think that it might have been what is now known as a dragon. It lurked in the deep river, and with its quick and powerful tail, it snatched unknowing passersby and gobbled them up. It was recounted that our ancestors, using a puppy as a bait, eventually killed the gigantic snake. Fearing that the dreaded reptile might have a mate that could come and exact vengeance, the people decided to desert the village. After many generations had passed, when the town was again being re-inhabited, a group of men were digging to build rice terraces when they uncovered crumbling potteries and traces of stone structures. It was the rediscovery of these ancient relics that led to the retelling of the long-forgotten story of the giant snake and the abandoned settlements.

"If it was really, really real, as Mercy's father claims, how come nobody saw the tabfiad?" I challenged Grandma.

"Why would our great-great-grandparents tell us if it was not real? Why would they deliberately lie to us? They simply passed on to us their stories, and we don't have to believe them if we don't want to." She spoke softly, her dreamy eyes staring at the horizon as she took a puff on her pipe and exhaled smoke leisurely.

We did not speak for a long while. We were both absorbed in our own thoughts. Then it occurred to me to ask her about what is real and what is not:

---

[5] A gigantic reptile with legs that devoured people and animals. It was also said to resemble a giant lizard because of its legs.

"Apu, please tell me what is *real*?"

She turned to look at me, but said nothing. Then she seemed to briefly scrutinize me with her eyes, from head to toe.

"What do you want to know?" she finally asked.

I asked her how one would know the truth – what a *real story* is.

"I will tell you the *truth*: A real story is the one you think or believe as a real story."

I was lost. I stared back at her, wide-eyed. She peered deeply into my eyes. Her eyes sparkled with delight as I watched her laugh.

"But I don't understand at all!" I blurted out, a little frightened and a little frustrated.

She was quiet for a while. She took her time preparing another bowl of tobacco. Then suddenly, she spoke even more enigmatically:

"There are many worlds, you know . . . *right here in our midst*. And that's why you saw the hu-lee gus." She winked at me.

"Do you remember that story of the hunter whose spear was swallowed by a quickmud in a little lake in the forest?" Grandma reminded me of another tale she had previously related to me.

The hunter was said to have been stalking a wild deer. He hurled his spear at the target, but the animal eluded it, and the spear fell and got stuck in a quickmud in a little lake. The hunter dove into the little lake to retrieve his spear, but he also sank in. It was accounted that he met people living under the earth, and these people did not have to hunt because animals abounded around them. He reported that the subterranean people's chickens and pigs were all white. When the people saw him, they said to him, "So are you the one nibbling at our animals?" To save his skin, he denied, saying, "No, it's not me." The underground villagers knew he wasn't telling the truth, but they still treated him well and invited him to live with them so he would not have to hunt anymore. But if he chooses to live with them, he will not be able to go back to the surface of the earth again. The hunter pondered their offer, but he missed his family and village, so he told them he wanted to go home. They directed him in the direction he should take to return to the earth's surface. He was said to have walked only a short distance when he came across a field of tall grasses. He waded through the tall grass until he reached a familiar location, at which point he knew exactly how to get back to his village. When the villagers saw him approaching, they asked where he had been as they had been all over searching for him for a month. He said he thought he had been away for only a day. He related his story about the subterranean villagers. This, according to Grandma, was how the people knew that there were also people living under the earth.

"Many worlds in our midst," Grandma again uttered, almost inaudibly, as if she was talking to herself.

Sensing my silence and befuddlement, she told me not to be so concerned, and to lighten up. She urged me to enjoy some of the biscuits I had brought for her. Then she tried to divert my attention away from my concern about what is real and what is not by telling me a new story – the story of the still water of a forbidden river called Kok.

The River Kok, according to her description, was very deep, dark, and still. The thickets on both sides of the river had grown over, blocking the sun from reaching areas near the river. Lichens had made the riverbank rocks slippery and moist. However, the stillness and the large concave shape of the river attracted children who loved to swim.

There was once a family with four children. The children consisted of three sisters and a baby brother who was just learning to walk. One day, the mother told the children to look after their baby brother so she could go to the fields and dig some sweet potatoes. She assured them that she would not be gone long and would be back as soon as she had dug enough potatoes. She told them that when the sun rises halfway across the sky and the water becomes warmer, they may go bathing in the spring nearby. She cautioned them against going down to the Kok River. The children assented, and their mother left. Soon after, their playmates arrived, inviting them to play together. After they had been playing for a while, they felt it was getting hot. One of the sisters suggested they go bathe in the spring. Their playmates, however, persuaded them to go swimming at the Kok. Forgetting their mother's words, they went down to the river. The eldest sister carried her baby brother on her back, and they all proceeded to Kok. As they reached their destination, the eldest sister sat her toddler brother under some bush shade, near shallow water. But they did not bathe as they again became engrossed in their playing. They were having so much fun digging holes in the sand and building little stone walls that they did not notice the toddler crawling towards the water. He saw a pine cone floating round and round on the surface of the quiet pool of water. He crawled to reach for it, but his right foot slipped, and he fell into the deep water. He kicked and struggled and gasped for air. When the older children heard his cries, they jumped into the water to pull him out. The eldest sister was able to get hold of him. She clasped her baby brother and hurried to bring him home. The other children followed her, and while they were climbing the protruding stone steps of the rice terrace, the second sister looked back to see where the baby had slipped. She was very frightened to see that the water was no longer still, but was now rapidly moving downstream.

"To this day, the water runs fast in the Kok because the baby kicked the stagnant water, but before that incident, the water did not flow, so debris, pinecones, rotten leaves, wild berries, and even dust gathered and got stuck and stale on the surface, endlessly going round and round and round." Grandma emphasized what she meant with a gesture of her index finger, outlining an imaginary circular motion in the air. "But now, when you see the River Kok, the water is rushing boisterously downstream, as if bragging about its newfound freedom."

Grandma paused and gently peered into my eyes. She was smiling, as amused as I was. Then she went on to tell me the moral of the story:

"A stagnant position is dangerous; movement is natural; don't get stuck going round and round and round in an aimless circle." She paused, and we again sat in complete silence.

"What happened to the baby?" I asked after a while.

"He died," she replied.

"Is it a real story?" I asked, widening my eyes in a false display of surprise.

"Of course it is!" Grandma roared, also widening her eyes to match my antics. She rapped her knuckles on my brow in amusement.

"If you don't believe me, go ask my cousin, your Apu Arfun, who lives alone like a hermit in Kok." She spoke emphatically, exaggeratedly lifting her arm in a sweeping motion, pointing in the direction of Kok.

We were again quiet. I imagined the River Kok and the children in the story. Then I further probed Grandma. I asked her where exactly the story of the hunter who was swallowed by the quickmud took place. She pointed to the farthest bluish mountain visible across the horizon to our right. Then she added that somewhere hidden in those misty mountains is also the lake where the seven beautiful celestial sisters come to play and swim when the moon turns into a big-round-rock (full moon).

We sat there in silence for a very long time. As I gazed towards the opalescent faraway mountains where some of the tales were supposed to have happened, I had the strangest sensation: the characters in Grandma's stories seemed to come alive. Certainly not with my physical eyes, but through some other sense, I *saw* the characters doing what they were doing as described in Grandma's stories. Their activities seemed to unfold concurrently, as if they were taking place at the present moment and not in some distant past. They did appear to have an older way of doing things, and they were garbed in different clothing, but it did not appear as if their time was past and gone. I distinctly felt that their usual activities were occurring precisely at the same moment that I was breathing, and that we were breathing the same air! It was as if we coexisted at the same time but, perhaps, in a different imaginary space – if we can speak of such a thing.

I was enjoying the fascinating multidimensional sensation, and then, I blinked – and caught myself back – to reality! Sitting next to me was Grandma, still smoking her pipe. Beneath us stretched the valley of green fields. On the opposite mountain, there stood my house and my elementary school.

I peeked at Grandma. She was preoccupied with her own thoughts and did not pay attention to me. I wanted to tell her what I *saw* – that uncanny, inexplicable sensation of seeing her tales come alive. But nothing came out of my mouth. I lacked the verbal ability to describe the vision. I surmised that I might have actually nodded off a bit, even while sitting upright, just like Grandma sometimes did, and had had a dream. The phenomenon had the feel of a dream – although I knew it was not a dream.

Those would be my last moments with Grandma as she passed away shortly after that conversation on what is real and what is not.

8

THE UNBELIEVERS

Mother was sitting in a chair knitting recycled yarn. She said she would make me a warm blanket for the cold nights we would spend on our distant farm in the middle of the forest. Mother asked me to sit on the floor so she could continue telling me the story of Moses while she knitted my blanket. My task, meanwhile, was to ward off the cat, which was always eager to play with the ball of yarn.

Moses, according to Mother, was a prophet chosen by God to lead His people out of slavery in Egypt and back to the Holy Land that God had promised them. Since their journey from Egypt to the Promised Land took a very long time, the story of Moses was also a very long tale, full of interesting twists and turns, awe-inspiring miracles, squabbles among themselves, and battles against the Gentiles.

"But you said, just a moment ago, that when they passed by the Mountain of Sinai, God gave them a commandment that they should not kill? Why did the Israelites kill all the men, women, children, and even animals as they reached the Holy Land?" I pointed out to Mother what I thought was an inconsistency in her story.

"Because the Israelites are God's chosen people, while the people who were occupying the Holy Land at that time were Philistines and Gentiles. The Philistines and Gentiles were sinners, and so they had to be driven out of the Holy Land. They were impure, pagans, who were worshiping many different gods."

"They were Unbelievers?"

"Yes, they were Unbelievers."

"Are we Israelites?"

"No, we are not."

"Are we Philistines?"

Mother slowed down her knitting and thought for a moment. At that moment, Father was passing by, and, overhearing my question, he roared:

"We are *Igorots*!" He laughed to himself as he went to the kitchen.

"Ma, are we Philistines?" I repeated.

"No, we are not," she said.

"What are we?"

Silence.

I wondered which group of people I belonged to. I prodded Mother:

"If we are not Israelites, not Philistines, what are we?"

"I think we . . . we are Gentiles ......" Mother stammered. She seemed very reluctant to say it.

"We are?" I grimaced in astonishment.

I could not have expected us to be Gentiles, because Gentiles, according to Mother, are Unbelievers, and Unbelievers are sinners!

"So God does not like us then?" I asked with a mixed note of disappointment and concern.

"What makes you think like that?" Mother asked.

"You've said that God favored the Israelites, and He disliked the Philistines, and also the Gentiles, because they are Unbelievers."

Mother stopped knitting and rested her hands on her lap. After a while, she said that we are neither Israelites nor Philistines, and that we are Gentiles, but we are Believers.

"Oh, are we a different kind of Gentiles?"

Mother did not respond. She resumed her knitting, avoiding my gaze.

"What will happen to us, Ma? Are we going to go to hell?"

"Does God like the Igorots? What about us, Igorots?" Father casually commented as he came back from the kitchen munching a sweet potato.

I looked at Mother, expectant of an answer to mine and Father's questions. Her brows were slightly contracted; she had a melancholic expression on her face. She ignored Father and reflectively answered my question with a question:

"Maybe God likes us since He gave us life. As long as we behave and obey His Commandments, so that we do not go to hell?"

Then she cautioned me not to be thinking too much, or my head would grow abnormally large and break.

"You go and feed the chicken before it gets dark. Go, go!" she ordered with urgency.

I sprung to my feet and went to the kitchen where I fetched some cooked sweet potatoes for the already raucous flock of chickens gathered in the yard, eagerly awaiting their evening ration.

9

THE KINGDOM OF HEAVEN

As the years went by, I found myself increasingly alone, and I turned to reading to fill up my time. There was, however, nothing much to read. There was only Mother's huge Bible, some Christian magazines, and a few comic magazines collected by my brothers. Our public school offered no other books apart from the limited government textbooks we faithfully browsed every day. Fortunately, the dearth of books was partially filled by a Christian non-governmental organization that came to my hometown to translate the Bible into the local vernacular. This NGO put up a small library from a collection of used books donated by Christian families from other places. At first, I borrowed the books from the library and had Mother read and relate the stories to me. Then, as I became more proficient, I read and reread the books myself.

The Bible storytelling sessions that entertained little children no longer gathered us around Mother. The Bible storytelling then progressed into a regular Bible study, which was attended by at least a couple of neighborhood ladies who came to our house to read and discuss the Words of God. Despite Mother coaxing Sainoc and Samier to join in, the two already grown teenagers did not find reading and discussing the Bible, interesting. Mother, nonetheless, especially required me to be present during these Bible studies. She believed that all the answers to my questions could be found in the Bible.

There were times when, after the neighborhood women had left, Mother would pensively share with me other things about God that deeply confounded her, which, in turn, added to my own increasing number of questions. One important concern of hers was *the key* to the kingdom of heaven. She was perplexed as to what Jesus meant when He said, *What you lose on earth will be lost in heaven*[6]. She thought if it meant that what she did not have here on earth, she would not also have in heaven. This concerned her because she saw herself lacking in many things on earth, and could it possibly mean that what she lacked on earth and had hoped to find in heaven would not, after all, be made available to her in heaven? Mother believed that a Christian's ultimate goal was *ascension* to heaven, where the promise of paradise, or God's kingdom, is to be found. However, that cryptic passage in Matthew 16:19, repeated at 18:18, disturbed her sublime notions about heaven. I, too, wondered if it indeed meant that what I did not have here on earth, I would not also have in heaven. It is simply bad news.

Another Bible story that caught Mother's imagination was about the Resurrection, in which Jesus would return and Satan would be bound and locked in the abyss. When this time comes, the Believers will be raised from the dead to reign with Jesus Christ for a thousand years[7]. During this time of Jesus' reign, all would be well because Satan would no longer be allowed to make sinners out of people. Mother was pinning all her faith in that future time, when the Messiah would return and rule for a Thousand Years.

---

[6] The actual passage in Matthew 16:19 is "I will give you the keys of the kingdom of heaven; whatever you bind on earth will be bound in heaven, and whatever you loose on earth will be loosed in heaven." And Matthew 18:18 says, "I tell you the truth, whatever you bind on earth will be bound in heaven, and whatever you loose on earth will be loosed in heaven." Apparently, Mother, whose English did not reach a scholarly level, understood the passage as far as her understanding of the English language could allow. She understood "loose" to mean "lose." She interpreted the passage according to her subjective understanding at that time. Not knowing any better, I, too, understood it the way she interpreted and related it to me then.

[7] Revelation 20:2-5 New International Version.

10

FREEDOM TO CHOOSE

My hometown's public school required one hour of catechism per week. An episode that deeply etched itself in my memory was the catechist's impassioned tale about how the Lord Almighty vanquished the Devil Lucifer.

"The Lord, in His great might and ultimate power, struck out bad Lucifer from heaven and flung him and his followers down to the eternal burning fires of hell."

According to Mr. Topia, the prim and proper catechist, hell is a lake of fire where all sinners go.

"Those condemned to hell will be very thirsty, yet they are not allowed to drink even a droplet of water. They gnash their teeth and cry all day and all night in agony, yet nobody will come and comfort them."

As ten-year-old kids, we were deeply impressed by God's superpower. Yet at the same time, we also became fearful of Him and this scary place where He casts those who are disobedient and proud, like Lucifer. With his head slowly shaking sideways, a menacing look in his eyes, and index finger wagging in admonition, Mr. Topia appeared to threaten when he proclaimed, "And the Lord Almighty sees and knows everything. No matter how hard you try, you can never run away and hide your sins from Him!"

"He sees even when we go to the loo?" one naughty boy asked.

"Of course!" Mr. Topia snapped, looking very irritated by the question.

"Iyay!" a girl sitting in the corner, remarked.

♥ ♥ ♥

That vivid incident with Mr. Topia, back when I was in fourth grade, later inspired me to ask a deeper question:

"Ma, why did God make such a bad angel as Lucifer?"

"God created Lucifer, a very beautiful and brilliant angel, but because of his beauty and brilliance, Lucifer thought he was as powerful as God, so he became a conceited rebel, and God punished him by throwing him to hell, where he now lives as the leader of all fallen angels."

"Yes, but you and Mr. Topia both said that God is so powerful that He knows and sees everything. Did He not know about the evil schemes of Lucifer?"

"Lucifer, *like us*, was given the freedom to choose or do whatever he wanted," Mother answered.

I had already heard of this 'freedom to choose' contention when I asked Mother why God did not confiscate the bad apple from Eve when He saw that she was about to eat it. And, if God truly sees and knows everything, why did He not prevent Eve from offering the forbidden fruit to Adam? Mother's explanation was that our first parents were given the freedom to choose what to do.

I have pondered a lot about Mother's explanation, only to come up with the opinion that what God really gave Adam and Eve was the *freedom to sin*. And in their ill-fated sinning, we inherited their fault. After I learned about the concept of Original Sin, it bothered me that the Original Sin of Adam and Eve was still attached to me after all those thousands of years that had passed since they first disobeyed and ate the forbidden fruit. Mother had then assured me that my Original Sin was removed after I was baptized to become a Christian by Father Norberto.

Therefore, having already contemplated the notion of freedom to choose, my response to Mother was ready. I told her that if God had not given freedom to choose to Lucifer, the latter would not have chosen to go against God's Will, and would not have had the freedom to cause all the bad people to sin. If Lucifer had been denied the freedom to choose, he would also have been denied the freedom to tempt Adam and Eve – and so we would not be, in the first place, carrying the Original Sin. I asked Mother why God gives us the freedom to choose, but then punishes us if we choose not to follow His rules and regulations.

Mother fell silent upon hearing my thoughts. She quietly washed off the brown earth sticking to the taro roots she dug up from the fields earlier that day. I was sitting on a chair in front of the hearth, waiting for the rice to boil so I could remove the pot cover and let the steam escape. After a while, Mother responded to my question by saying that she was not really very sure about the case of Lucifer. She told me to better ask Mr. Topia, the catechist, or Tomas, my elder brother who converted to become a Baptist.

Mother was very disappointed with my big brother, Tomas, who doubted the Catholic persuasion and joined the Baptist legion. She received harsh criticism from Father Norberto and her other Catholic friends for allowing, albeit unwillingly, one of her children to stray to the rival religion in our small town. Despite Father Norberto and her Catholic friends' incitements, Mother was unable to convince my brother to return to the Catholic faith. So Mother was left with no choice but to acquiesce to Tomas' freedom to choose what to do.

Now that Mother had urged me to ask my Baptist brother my questions, I didn't think it was a good idea. I have observed that my brother was aggressive in promoting and defending his beliefs, which he claimed are what the Bible really says. When I was very young, in the deep of the night, I would often hear Mother and Tomas arguing about their differing religious beliefs or interpretations of the Bible. Their loud discussions would wake me up from my sleep, and there were times when their intense arguments so deeply disturbed me that I could not go back to sleep. Lying very still, resting my head on Mother's lap pretending to be fast asleep, I listened, quietly, to everything they had to say about God. One time, I asked Mother why she always argued with Tomas about Jesus, and why Tomas became very serious and preached as if he were Father Norberto. Mother's response was that it was because my big brother had become a fanatic. I asked what it means to become a 'fanatic'. Fanatics, according to Mother, are those who are absolutely convinced that their point of view is always correct.

It was then that I became deeply perplexed, as I was already deeply intrigued by God. There were times when I wondered whether Mother was also becoming a fanatic like Tomas. Meanwhile, I felt intimidated by my big brother, and I never dared to ask him any of my questions.

11

CLASH OF WORLDS

It was in college, when I was asked to help with research on herbal medicines and traditional healers in rural areas, that I came to learn how Mother was Christianized. For the research, I interviewed Mother about Apu, who was a traditional healer. The interview took us back to some of Mother's past, which I had not known until that time.

Mother was born inside a grass-roofed, soot-painted, one-room wooden house pitched firmly on the hardened earth at the edge of a hilltop in the farthest village in town. She said her family was very poor. During the cold season, they endured the cold mountain climate with scant clothing and a few pieces of handwoven rough blankets. For heating at night, they relied on the fire on the hearth, which was kept burning all night. Mother had two younger sisters and a younger brother. Mother's father worked in the fields and also hunted, just like the other men in the village at that time. Her mother, my grandma, was also an ordinary subsistence farmer, but in addition, she healed people of their sickness. I learned from Mother that when Grandma was not yet too old to perform her healing rituals, she made use of plants, feathers, amulets, stories and prayers. She summoned spirits and went into trance – a process which, according to Mother, often jolted Grandma's small and fragile frame.

About twelve years before Mother was born, Christian missionaries started to arrive. The first group of missionaries introduced Catholicism, the first of the three early Christian groups that penetrated the village-town. When Mother was growing up, children, especially, were encouraged to attend the catechisms held in the evenings at the convent. The convent and the church were conveniently built at the center of the town, in a narrow valley by the river. They referred to these catechisms as *sos-oron Apu Dios*, or 'teachings of God'. The very first catechists were the first foreign priests. Later on, catechists were recruited from the ranks of earlier converts from the lowlands.

To attend the evening catechisms, Mother and her younger sisters burned resinous pine torches to light their path as they descended the mountain to go to the convent in the valley to listen to the 'teachings of God'. In every attendance, they were each given a ticket or coupon. At the end of a certain period, they turn in their accumulated tickets in exchange for used clothing. A thicker collection was exchanged for thicker clothing, and a thinner or less collection was exchanged for thinner clothing.

Mother was confronted with an alternative reality as a result of the new religion. Aside from the material incentive it provided, which was both a necessity and a novelty for them at the time, the new religion piqued Mother's deep curiosity about other people and cultures. It infused her with new dreams and hopes for a better life – a life different from what her parents lived and believed.

"Did Apu ever prevent you and your sisters from going to listen to the teachings of God?" I asked.

"No, she did not," Mother answered retrospectively. "I only remember once or twice during a downpour or typhoon when *Ina*[8] asked if my sisters and I may not go to the convent that evening."

"So she gave you freedom to choose," I said, smiling.

"I guess so," she smiled back.

Within a decade of the Catholic Church's establishment, the

---

[8] Mother

public primary school was put up by the Americans. The Americans were also the very first teachers. Later, lowlanders who had long been Christianized took over the teaching in the school. The school worked in tandem with the Church to evangelize, "straighten out," and *save* what they believed were the crooked and wayward lost souls of the non-Christian tribes.

Unlike many of the other village children who had to be coaxed, and even forced by the authorities to go to school, Mother herself was more than eager to go to school. Even though her family house was the farthest from school, as much as she had the chance, she attended school.

After graduating from the free primary school in our hometown, Mother wanted so much to continue her formal schooling and reach at least the secondary level. But secondary school was neither free nor available in the village-town nor in any bigger town nearby. So Mother kept her dreams to herself as she went about her daily village life, helping her family in the fields. But having been captivated by exotic Bible stories and influenced by her interaction with school teachers and catechists from outside the village-town, Mother's consciousness wandered, drifted, far beyond the humdrum of ordinary village life. She wondered, and fantasized, about the people and places that lay behind the tall mountains tightly sequestering her small village-town from the rest of the world.

Eventually, at the age of sixteen, she decided to follow her dreams. She traveled to the city and sought to live with an aunt who had earlier moved to the city and was earning a living by buying and selling vegetables at the city market. Even as her busy, business-minded aunt did not honor the Sabbath day, Mother, alone, regularly went to Mass at the city cathedral. Then her prayers were heard, and her wishes were granted.

At the cathedral, she met a certain lady, the wife of a modern doctor. It turned out that this lady was as religiously devoted as she was. The lady had been looking for somebody to help take care of her small children, and she thought God had answered her prayers when she found Mother. She took Mother to live with her family as a household help. The lady's family lived in a huge house with many rooms. Mother's new benefactor, whom she affectionately called 'mom', became her version of a wish-granting godmother. Instead of paying her wages, her mom decided to send her to school for half-days while she worked the rest of the day. Mother was then enrolled in a private Catholic school located directly across the street from her employer's front door. Although Mother was already baptized back in the village, to make sure that she was 'properly' baptized, her mom arranged another baptism ceremony for her. Mother's mom stood as her sponsor and Christian godmother. Her prayers to God, heard; her dream to continue studying in school, granted; and, being double-baptized, Mother's Catholic Christian faith was solidified.

After living several years in the city, the news that her father had fallen ill prompted Mother to visit her family back in the village. She related to me the episode of her homecoming:

Tired and exhausted from her long journey from the city to the village, what met her eyes as she stepped into her family's front yard stunned her. She saw a scruffy girl in a dainty white dress sitting on an old wooden trunk, winnowing rice grains. It was her youngest sister. She was wearing Mother's most precious, special dress – the immaculate white baptismal dress – a gift from Mother's godmother, which Mother had earlier sent home, reserved, supposedly for her little sister's use, on that 'special day' when the latter would also, finally, be baptized to become a 'true Christian'. A scruffy girl in that special white dress against the backdrop of an old, grass-roofed, soot-painted, four-cornered little wooden hut adjacent to a dug-out stinking pigpen was not quite right – it was an abomination, as far as Mother was concerned. Infuriated, Mother yelled at her unknowing little sister, yelling that the white dress should only be worn to church after thoroughly cleaning oneself of soot and grit. Startled, the little sister dropped the winnower, scattering all the rice grains across the yard. Mother was cursing and mumbling at what she said was her sister's utter ignorance when Apu emerged from the hut's little door and calmly asked her to forgive her little sister's misdemeanor. Apparently, the white baptismal dress held loads of sacred sentiments for Mother, and it was, unfortunately, sacrilegiously out of place in the overall picture of that moment.

After the years spent away from home, Mother was appalled, and saddened, by the stark contrast between her refined and affluent city environment and the rugged and rudimentary village setting she had once left behind. This deeply disturbed her, as she could not reconcile the two different worlds: the world where she came from and the world she wanted to be in. She correlated her family's poverty with animism, or paganism, and the wealth of her benefactors in the city with Christianity.

Mother completed her secondary education. Although her godmother wanted to send her to college, her home situation had such an impact on her that she chose to forego college and return home to the village instead. She told me that although her parents did not stop her from leaving home to pursue the life she wanted, the 'spiritual destiny' of her family became her top priority. Her father eventually passed away. The image of her unbaptized father burning in hell constantly haunted her imagination. She worried that her heathen mother would also pass away, spiritually unprepared. All that she now wanted was to prevent her mother from following her father to hell. She worried that her younger siblings would follow their mother's unchristian ways.

The fear of hell was deeply implanted in Mother's psyche. She was single-minded, and she made it her personal mission and duty to bring God and the Christian Ways to her family and village people.

Mother married Father and, with relative success, raised one big

Christian family. Mother was very involved in the local Catholic church and, for some time, before I was born, she also served as the town parish catechist. Though less assiduous than her, Mother's two younger sisters followed in her footsteps and became Catholic Christian devotees. She was also able to have her youngest brother baptized, though he had no interest in religion or churchgoing and thus remained a free-spirit skeptic. Mother only had one problem left to deal with – her *ina*. Grandma's continuing practice of the old ways constantly challenged Mother's peace of mind.

One decisive day, unable to wait any longer, fearful that her now very old mother would die at any time, and spiritually unprepared, Mother went up the mountain to Grandma's hut and declared that she herself would baptize Grandma to finally become a Christian.

"Did Apu refuse to be baptized?" I asked.

"No, she didn't. She remained calm and quiet."

"How did you baptize her?"

"I told her to kneel. I poured holy water on her head and prayed over her in the name of Jesus that she would repent, be forgiven of all her sins, and become a Believer of God and the Christian Ways."

"Why didn't the Belgian priest of our town, at that time, baptize her instead of you?"

"Because the priest was too old to go up the mountain, and Ina made an excuse that she was also too old to go down to the valley."

"Why did you have to baptize her, and perhaps against her will?"

"Because she had been an Unbeliever."

"A pagan Gentile?"

"Yes."

I became quiet. I thought of Apu. Something was not quite right about Mother's behavior towards her – it was an abomination, as far as I was concerned. At the time of the interview with Mother, I was already a nineteen-year old idealistic college student. Although Mother had raised me a Christian, I had been having life experiences of my own that impelled me to entertain skepticism about many things I had previously been taught.

"So Apu was an uncivilized savage? A condemned sinner?"

I could not hide my own growing contempt towards Mother's condemnation of Grandma.

"I had the best of intentions. I wanted Ina's soul to be saved," Mother responded with a sulky look on her face.

"Saved from what, again?" I asked, sarcastically.

"From the Devil's clutches," she replied.

"So you seriously believe that your father, your grandparents, your great-grandparents, and all our ancestors who lived before the Christians made us believe that we are sinners and God-condemned people are all eternally burning in a lake of fire?"

"I don't know......" Mother spoke softly with a heavy sigh.

She stared down at the floor. I could tell that it was painful for her to imagine that her beloved unbaptized father and doting grandparents were eternally being tortured in hell.

"But I think Grandmother, Grandfather, and our ancestors were good people; even if they had flaws, could they have been any worse than the Christians who brought Christianity to our country and made slaves of our countrymen? They who came and burned our villages to the ground after stealing our power objects?"

Her eyes downcast, Mother did not say anything. *It was now my turn to tell her stories* – stories I learned in school, stories I read from scholarly books. I told her about the clever use of religion to legitimize the so-called *Divine Mission* of the colonizers to invade and occupy our country. I told her how the colonizers convinced their own people that, through *Divine Providence*, God gave them "special strength," "special leadership," and "moral responsibility," referred to as the *White Man's Burden*, to civilize and Christianize what they deemed was the rest of the savage world. I explained to her how the colonizers believed, and how they made us believe, that as a more advanced and superior race, it was their "moral obligation" to elevate our purportedly lower level status to that of their alleged illustriousness and superiority in morality, culture, and civilization. I told her how, in 1904, the Americans brought more than a hundred Igorots to North America to be exhibited at the St. Louis Exposition in order to display to the American public the "wild tribes" of the Philippines. Throughout the entire exposition, the unique Igorot tribesmen and women, marketed as "rare specimens of savage people," drew the largest crowds and earned profitable income for the event organizers. They were, however, made to live in inhumane conditions. The wages promised to them were not paid, and they were *forced* to butcher and eat dog meat every day just to showcase how 'nasty' and 'brutish' they were, *as a race*. This display was political propaganda devised by conniving politicians and businessmen whose deeper agenda was to *justify* the U.S. Government's colonization of the entire Philippines – allegedly with the benevolent intention of civilizing us, the backward people.[9]

Mother remained mournfully quiet.

"Yes, Ma, it was us – the Igorot people – notorious to the Spaniards as the 'infidels sitting on mountains of gold', who were specifically handpicked by the Americans to be used to justify their

---

[9] Howard T. Fry, A History of the Mountain Province (Quezon City: New Day Publishers, 1983), 39-41.

takeover colonization from Spain, so they could wrest the gold mines from us, a very important prospect the Spanish conquistadors repeatedly failed to accomplish, as they were unable to outdo the resistance of our people."

I made it clear to Mother that what I was telling her was based on research and an analytical study of history, and thus it is the *real deal story*.

Mother remained quiet. Since she did not utter any comment, I wondered if she understood my long talk after all. So I related to her another real story that occurred right at home. A very rarely told story, a so-called taboo story discreetly related to me by an old man whom I had interviewed for a required paper in my history class. The old man related to me a story about a group of villagers who were treacherously murdered in an unceremonious, savage way:

A detachment of Spanish soldiers, accompanied by native guides from hostile villages, trekked to our hometown and camped on a hilltop overlooking the village-town. They sent words of promise that they had come in peace and would not fight the natives. They invited the people of the villages to go up the hill so they could talk and make friends. But the villagers were wary of the strangers, as the latter had previously burned down the whole village-town during their earlier attempts to subdue the people. The villagers were also not oblivious to the unpleasant fate of the lowland towns that were already under direct colonial control. So they ignored the Spaniards and went about their daily lives, hoping that the conquistadors would soon get bored and leave. It was not until several weeks had passed, and with the foreign soldiers' persistent invitation, that some villagers went up the hill with food and water as peace offerings, believing that the conquistadors would honor their own words. Upon reaching the conquistadors' camp, however, the villagers were nabbed, tied down, and became the butt of jokes and insults for the Spaniards' entertainment. The

Spaniards took pleasure in scraping the skin from their buttocks and legs, then tossing the scraped skin over the fire to be grilled. Then, believing that the mountain tribes were headhunting cannibals, the conquistadors forced the villagers to swallow their own barbecued skins. The Spaniards left them to slowly bleed to death.

"Isn't such an act barbaric and savage more than anything else known and heard of in these mountains?" I asked, looking straight at Mother.

Mother stared back at me, aghast. I do not know if her shocked reaction was the result of hearing that gruesome story for the first time, or because, without any inhibition, I disregarded a prohibition by recounting a forbidden story. But she made no attempt to contest the truthfulness or accuracy of the account. She remained speechless.

A method of very slow, deliberate torture to death, like what was done to the villagers, was bizarre and unheard of. It was considered taboo or forbidden to recount such a tragic incident, which, at that time, was seen as a disgrace – an ill-omened event that had befallen not only the actual victims, but their whole extended family – affecting the fortunes of their departed ancestors as well as their future unborn generations. Moreover, an inauspicious event such as that has tarnished the honor of a whole, proud, warrior tribe traditionally known for their fierceness and dexterity in battle. Certainly, tribal battles among the Igorots were fought with what would now be considered crude weapons such as spears and head axes, but for these mountain warrior societies, who observed their own unspoken codes of warfare, the best of the warriors were recognized and commended for their skill at finishing off an opponent with a single strike, sparing the fallen from unnecessary pain.

I told Mother that, like her good intentions to save Grandma's soul, however divinely sanctioned and benevolent the Christian conquerors' intentions may have been, their ways of civilizing the uncivilized are, ironically, what is considered the savage way, as far as our people are concerned. I told her that Divine Mission it might have been through the *righteous eyes* of the invaders, it was an Evil Mission, as far as the recipients of the Mission were concerned.

After a very long, uneasy silence, Mother tried to veer us back to our original topic:

"Although they were good people, our ancestors died without being baptized. And those who die without being baptized in the name of Jesus Christ, are carrying with them the Original Sin," Mother explained weakly.

"I heard that the people inhabiting the mountains behind the highest peak of our town have innumerable gods and goddesses; are you sure that all these folks are going to march to a lake of fire when Judgment comes?"

"*Anak,*[10] you have to understand, God is a jealous God. Remember his First Commandment? He does not want us to worship other gods before Him."

"Right on! If God, Himself, is convinced that He is the only God, then who is He jealous of?"

"Against the false gods, pretender gods."

A gloomy silence supervened. Mother's expression remained despondent. Finally, as she let go of another heavy and weary sigh, she said, "We don't know the *Will of God*, my child."

---

[10] Child

12

THE WILL OF GOD

When I was fifteen, Father died. He suffered from a stroke, then after about a year's treatment in and out of the hospital, he succumbed to complications. Compared to Grandma's peaceful passing, Father's death came as an unexpected blow to me. I abruptly stopped going to church. Adolescence issues and troubles in school added to my grief. I slipped into a deep, dark teenage depression.

A face-distorting and starvation-inducing toothache, though painful and unasked for, conveniently excused me from going to school for a while and from dealing with members of my family. I locked myself up in my room. Days in pain and seclusion, however, left me with nothing much to do but to bury myself deeper into dark, morose, self-pitying, self-blaming thoughts. Life came to feel excruciatingly painful, unreasonable, unfair, meaningless and random. Night and day, I lay languidly in bed, staring at the ceiling, asking countless questions with no known answers. Was I a good daughter while he was alive? Why did Father have to die when he was much needed by the family, regarded for his work in the community, while a sick, nobody like me is left to live and suffer from physical pain, emotional anguish and mental torture? Why did I not die instead of him? What is the point of life? These and a hundred more questions whirled through my head until I got exhausted and cried myself to sleep – only to wake up and be reminded of them again.

♥ ♥ ♥

Bloody streaks of red-orange clouds trailed the dark orange sun as it slid quietly behind the mountains. I had just emerged from my days of self-imposed seclusion. I found Mother sitting on the balcony. She was contemplatively and contentedly reading her few collections of *Our Daily Bread* and *The Plain Truth* magazines. I sat on a low wooden bench beside her chair and asked a question that startled her.

"Ma, why was I born?"

"What do you mean?" She looked at me in a manner that was as if my question did not deserve to be asked.

"I don't know . . . but what am I born for? What are we born for?" I asked, somberly.

"Do you not like to have been born?" Mother lifted her brows, widening her eyes in a probing manner.

I hesitated and looked away, not quite sure of how to express my sentiments. Mother's raised brows dropped into a knit, perplexed at what I was up to.

I let go of a weary, quivering deep breath and, in a grave, forceful tone, I blurted out the painful question I had been asking myself over and over again:

"Look Ma, we were born, we grow up, we go to school, we argue and get insulted in school, we marry, we raise children, we work very hard, we get sick, we suffer, and then – we die – just like Father. What is it all for?" I asked with utmost sincerity, almost begging her to tell me the answer to the mystery of life.

Mother opened her mouth to speak, but her vocal cords refused to deliver. After a very long inconvenient pause, she painfully stammered, "I . . . I don't know. . . . I wish I knew. I don't know God's Will." Her brows remained contracted; she avoided my gaze; her eyes, beleaguered.

"But Ma, you gave birth to me! I did not wish to be born!" My frustration turned into a muffled scream.

Mother was shocked.

"What am I going to do? Cut up my stomach and put you back in there!" she wailed. A sharp, defensive look flared in her eyes as she looked down, ferociously at me.

I was taken aback by her emotional outpouring. It was my turn to be shocked. I started to weep.

"No, I just wanted to know, or I'd rather be dead!" My tone was strong and threatening as I flashed her a sharp, defiant glance. My insinuation of suicide angered and frightened her even more.

"You ungrateful child!" she shrieked as she raised her open palm to slap me. Her hand stopped short of hitting me; instead, she caught and cupped my face with both hands:

"My child, aren't you glad that I brought you here?" she asked, imploringly.

She looked straight into my eyes. By the look in her eyes, I could tell that she was hurt and desperate. I wept some more. I felt very sorry for upsetting her, but I was, at the same time, very angry. I was also hurt and desperate.

The sun had completely sunk beneath the mountains. A gloomy silence took over. Despite the noisy chatter of evening insects, an oppressive, deafening stillness abounded between me and Mother. My cat, who seemed to have felt the tension, jumped onto my lap; it positioned itself comfortably and then sympathetically joined us in the silence. The warmth of the cat and its rhythmic purring infused some life and warmth into my stiff and cold body. I petted the cat and thanked it in my mind. Its greenish eyes, sharp and luminous in the dark, glanced up at me and meowed once, as if to acknowledge my gratitude. I felt shivers go down my spine.

Mother broke the chilly silence:

"Why don't you instead read the Bible and learn about the teachings of God? Because, I have to admit, I don't know all the answers myself." Without looking at me, she spoke in an apologetic, reconciliatory manner.

"I did. I've been reading the Bible a lot lately, but I didn't find an answer. Instead, it just confirmed what I already knew."

"What did it say?" Mother's face lit up.

"It said that life is utterly meaningless, that what happened before will happen again, and it will go on like that in a cycle. It said that there is nothing new under the sun. The author, who was said to be a very wise king, mentioned that an unborn child who has not yet seen evil is even in a better position than one who has been born and seen evil, because both of them are destined to die, anyway. It said that *everything in life is meaningless, a chasing after the wind*. That was what it said in Ecclesiastes." I eloquently recounted to Mother what I read from my newest favorite chapter in the Bible.

Silence took over again. Mother sat motionless; her eyes fixed on the dark space in front of us. A melancholic frown was etched on her forehead. Her face was drawn and very pale in the dim light coming from inside the house.

"Anak, we have to have faith," she finally spoke.

"Faith in whom? Faith in what?"

"Faith in God."

"You mean, the God of the Israelites?"

Silence.

"Remember the story of Job?" she asked.

I remember the story of Job, the most God-fearing man in the Bible who had an infallible faith in God. God and Satan were playing a game of challenge. God asked Satan if he had noticed His servant Job, the most blameless and upright man on earth. Satan scoffed at God's claim, saying that Job would certainly remain loyal to God because the latter had made Job a very wealthy man. To prove his point, Satan proposed taking away Job's wealth, and the man would surely abandon God. Quite challenged, God permitted Satan to strip Job of his possessions, including his 10 children, but forbade Satan from taking the mortal's life. So, in an instant, Job lost all his children, servants, animals, and all his wealth. In spite of this great misfortune, Job did not turn away from God. And then again, God proudly announced to Satan that Job had remained blameless and upright despite Satan's inciting him against God, to the extent that Job's life was reduced to nothing, and for no justifiable reason at all. Satan refused to give in so easily. He contested God once more. Satan expressed that if Job's very existence were threatened, if he were confronted with his mortality, he would surely do all he could to save his skin. Again, God accepted the challenge. He told Satan to go ahead and do whatever he wanted to do to Job, as long as he didn't actually kill him. So Satan made Job sick. Job's body, from head to toe, was infested with painful sores. His friends found him sitting on the ground, scraping his sores with pieces of broken pottery. His wife and friends ridiculed him for hanging on to God, who appeared to have completely forsaken him. However, despite all these misfortunes, Job remained loyal and faithful to God. Hence, as a reward, God multiplied all that he had lost.

Job's story was one of my favorites as a child. Despite being tragic, it has a happy ever-after ending. As I grew older, however, the magic of the tale seemed to have waned. The feeling was likened to that of a growing child outgrowing a fairytale, or a progressing scholar outgrowing a previously appealing idea.

When I was younger and first heard the story of Job, I asked Mother why the almighty God did not, once and for all, simply eliminate His number one enemy – Satan or Lucifer – instead of allowing or inciting His Chosen People to kill the Philistines and pagan Gentiles as a way of getting even with the leader of these Unbelievers. Mother's answer had been that because Lucifer is a spirit, like God, he cannot be killed. I have wondered why God created spirit-Lucifer in the first place. Mother's answer had been that God created a beautiful and brilliant angel Lucifer, who, unfortunately, turned into a proud rebel. So I asked why God, who knows everything, would create a traitor angel like Lucifer. Mother's answer had been that Lucifer, *like us*, was given free will, or the freedom to choose what to do. I had contemplated in and out and around this idea of free will, and what I came up with was the suspicion that what God gave us and Lucifer was simply the *freedom to sin* because He gave us the *option* to do evil.

At first, Mother was baffled by my opinion about God giving us the freedom to sin. When she recovered from her bafflement, she vigorously shook her head in objection and contended that it could not possibly be that simple – that freedom to choose could not be the same as freedom to sin. Then she said that, unlike my naive but wild thinking, *God's Mind* does not work in such simplistic terms.

I then wondered how God's Mind works. I wondered why, in all His widely talked-about might and glory, God submitted to Satan's challenge, which only resulted in the torment of a human being like Job. I asked Mother why that was.

"So He will show the Devil how foolish he is to challenge God. And to show to all of us that after this and that has all been said and done, in the end, it is still the Will of God that prevails."

"But why does God have to allow human beings to suffer

enormously just to prove something to Satan? Punish and kill the enemies of the Believers just to make the point that He is the one and only?"

"So doubtful people like you will *hear a story* and believe in God's might and existence; listen then, if you have ears!" she exhorted.

I kept quiet, obviously unimpressed.

"Let's say that the story's purpose is to illustrate that no matter how troubled and miserable our life is, God will reward us, tenfold, if we hold on to Him until the end," Mother added.

Her looking at me askance made me feel like an irredeemable sinner.

The mortality of man, vividly exemplified by the prolonged suffering and eventual death of Father, led me to adopt an obstinate, cynical, fatalistic point of view. I thought that with such a degree of suffering borne by Job, he would have been better off dead – rather than alive, serving as a sacrificial example for God to prove a point to Satan. Because, in the end, after all was said and done between God and Satan, Job would end up a dead man anyway. I thought that a man alive is merely prolonging his sufferings – his mortal life being subject to the whimsical mercy of God and the mischief of Satan. Life, to me, came to become synonymous with suffering, and death, appeared to be the end of suffering. That is, of course, presuming that when I die, my soul will go to heaven rather than hell.

"What makes it different if I eat ten sacks of rice or a hundred? If I live eighteen years instead of eighty?" I mumbled under a weary sarcastic sigh.

"If you live longer, you will have more chances to enjoy your life," Mother answered, also wearily.

Did Father enjoy his life? Every day, he worked very hard. He always had many things going on in his mind to think about. One day, he suddenly fell off his chair and became unconscious. They flew him to the hospital in the city in a helicopter. After many months, my elder siblings brought me to the city to see him. I was appalled. I could not recognize my father! He was emaciated. He could not walk. His voice was garbled. He was confined to a wheelchair. I saw deep sadness and resignation in his eyes. He was clearly exhausted by what he had to go through. After enduring much pain, suffering, and a staggering medical bill that worried everyone in the family, death claimed him in the end anyway, in the middle of his fifth decade, perhaps even less than half of Grandma's age when she passed away.

"Are you enjoying your life, Ma?" I asked, after a while. Mother did not respond. The melancholic expression on her face remained. She dropped her gaze to the floor.

"What assurance do we have that we will enjoy and be happy in our lives if we live longer rather than shorter?" I asked again.

"If you live longer, you will have more opportunities to correct your mistakes, and thus you will have more chances of happiness," Mother responded.

"And if I live longer, I'll also have more chances of committing more mistakes, and thus more chances of unhappiness," I said.

"We live by faith. Through *God's Will* and *mercy*, we will be bestowed a good life," she replied.

God's Will? Faith? God's mercy? A good life? All at once, I was reminded of a piteous incident when I was little:

I watched as Mother rose from the ground. She looked despairingly towards heaven. Ruined crops dangled from her hands. She called out loud to God, asking why the merciful Creator created those 'insignificant' field mice who steal her crops, leaving nothing for her many pitiful children to eat. We waited for an answer from God, but none came. Grandma, who was resting at the farm shed, spoke instead. She told Mother that the sneaky mice who come to steal the crops at night are our shape-shifted dead ancestors of many generations past who periodically come to get their share of food. Grandma then wanted to tell Mother about the prayers to drive away the mice, but Mother vehemently scoffed at Grandma's pagan beliefs, dismissing them as purely demonic. Mother refused to hear any of Grandma's mouse-repelling remedies. Instead, she continued to sorrowfully look up towards heaven, hoping, pleading, for God to have mercy on us.

Because we are a big family, both Mother and Father worked very hard. And being Catholic, family planning to limit the number of children did not sound like a moral idea to them. I think if they had consciously decided to have fewer children, they would not have felt compelled to devote most of their lives toiling to provide for a big family. And ironically, I – the last child, and the one who did not wish to be born, would not be alive now, complaining and bemoaning over what I consider to be the misfortune of being born. I wondered if it was God, through His incomprehensible Will, who decided about my birth, Father's death, and so on. I felt helpless at the thought that events in people's lives are determined by God's Will.

"You know what's wrong with you? You're just starting out and you're already a coward. You're afraid to experience life." I heard Mother softly say as she noticed my long, broody silence.

Mother is wrong, a thought of protest sprang from within me. It's not that I am afraid to experience life; I just want to know what the point of life is. Why was I born? Why did Father die the way he did? What is God's Will?

I did not feel like further discussing the matter with Mother. When it comes to the mystery of God and His unfathomable Will,

Mother was a confused, tortured soul. Taking after her somber temperament and contemplative inclination, I, too, beginning at a tender age, was a confused, tortured soul. The only other people in the big family who bothered to delve into the mysteries of life and God, yet who did not appear to be confused at all, were Tomas and Grandma. Tomas and Grandma have appeared, to me, to have reached an enviable higher state of understanding that could not be budged. Compared to Mother who sometimes wavered, Tomas and Grandma were poised and confident in each of their own positions. I looked up to Tomas' youthful boldness and his show of strength of conviction. He was an idealistic, articulate, young man who had received a scholarship to study to become a pastor. Meanwhile, I was intrigued and drawn to Grandma's depth and mystery. Grandma and Tomas assessed each other with mixed feelings. Tomas had always regarded Grandma as an ignoramus, yet a very gentle and clever old woman. Grandma thought of Tomas as a fine young man of intelligence, but who needed 'to eat more rice' before he could gain a better understanding of the things he professed to know.

Mother tried once more, "If you live long enough, you'll have more chances to answer your questions; don't you like that?" She spoke on a more cheerful note, trying to cheer me up and engage back my interest.

I remained morosely silent. A scowl on my face.

"Perhaps we live to find out the answer to why we live?" she again added, thoughtfully.

We live to find out the answer to why we live? I thought it was a pretty funny idea – like a silly game thought up by a cruel trickster. But, as absurd as it may sound, I had to admit that such an idea is more enlightened than the belief that it is the Will of God that we live, and in the sorry manner that we do. But wouldn't it be wasted sacks of rice if I lived for eight decades and still had no idea why I lived? Because ironically, like what I observed in my parents' lives,

I would have been too busy procuring the sacks of rice that would sustain my day-to-day existence – rather than investigating the reason for my existence. Perhaps the earlier I discovered the reason for my existence, the more I would savor every morsel of the rice that I would be procuring.

Nothing more was spoken between Mother and me. We both stared at the blank darkness before us. That night, I noticed that even the sky was devoid of stars. I gently petted the cat, who had been patiently listening to our conversation. I did not doubt the existence of God, I thought. Surely, there must be a God who fashioned a very cute, loving, furry animal like a cat which also appeared to be highly intelligent. But then again, how does God's Mind work? This so-called Will of God that I too often hear Mother refers to when she runs out of answers?

The enigmatic Will of God appeared, to me, to be the greatest riddle, or puzzle, ever devised. I thought that perhaps when I finally come to decipher the Will of God, the rest of my questions and concerns in life will become trifles.

13

A SECRET

When I was about to finish my final year of secondary school, one evening after dinner, Mother announced that, for lack of money, she would not be able to send me to college. My heart sank upon hearing this unexpected news. My friends and I had been excitedly talking about college, and we were looking forward to going to the colleges in the city. It never occurred to me that I might not be able to attend college after all.

Our schoolteachers, in their efforts to encourage and inculcate in us the importance of education, had been telling us that without a college degree, we, indigenous people, would remain poor, ignorant, and easily duped. And that our lot would be limited to doing the hard work in the fields that our parents and grandparents have been doing all their lives. I felt depressed over the idea of becoming what my teachers imagined to be my destiny if I failed to get a college education. My eldest brother suggested that I go to the small government college in the provincial capital. He said that all schools are the same and that, in the end, all I need is a paper diploma certifying that I have completed a college degree.

That night, I went to my room feeling very dejected. Mother followed me to my room, a Bible in her hand. She sat on my bed and said that she was going to tell me a secret. But first, she reminded me of her circumstances when she was my age and was equally hopeful about continuing her formal schooling. More than me, she had to contend with greater challenges. The nearest place where she could obtain a secondary education was in the same city where I now wanted to study for college. During her time, this city was accessed through an unstable, narrow mountain road, which required travelers to trek for a number of days if their motor vehicle could not pass through due to bad weather. Initially, as going to school was very unpopular when she was young, it was inconceivable for her family to allow her to do more schooling, especially in a distant city. And how would her parents pay for her schooling when they did not even use money in their day-to-day lives? Most importantly, Mother was well aware that her family needed her more to help them in the fields rather than allowing her, as the eldest child, to pursue a dream whose significance they did not at all understand. Therefore, in her case at that time, the prospect of obtaining even a mere secondary education was very bleak, if not impossible.

Mother said that whenever she got the chance, she escaped into the world of fantasy. She often wished for some generous and kind people to help her go to school. She described to me how she vividly imagined and *created stories* in her mind:

"Every time I quietly pulled weeds in the fields, or was resting in between pounding rice grains, and every night, as I lay down to sleep, I saw myself in school. It was not anything like the rustic school in our town but a big, beautiful, white-walled school building just like the picture I saw on the catechist's postcard. I saw myself comfortably sitting at a desk, feeling the fine texture of paper between my thumb and index finger as I turned the pages of a musty-smelling book. I could smell the pungent metallic ink of a fountain pen as I wrote my name in beautiful cursive. I heard the rough sound of chalk hitting and sliding across the chalkboard as my teacher wrote a song. I savored seeing these kinds of scenes in my mind over and over again, and I felt very happy."

Daydreaming, according to Mother, had been a spontaneous and unconscious past time for her. She said that since there were no radios, movies, and many other things when she was young, she entertained herself by creating her own stories and movies in her mind. She claimed that she did not have any clue that the scenes she had been conjuring in her imagination would, someday, happen, almost exactly as she had seen them in her mind's eye.

"My godmother found me and enrolled me in a big, beautiful school with white walls." Mother spoke retrospectively as she reminisced about the past. Then she told me, in a low voice, that we should keep her 'confession' a secret.

I asked why it should be a secret. She said it was because it is a pagan practice. I asked her which one was a pagan practice.

After a reflective pause, she talked, hesitatingly, about Grandma. Mother said that since she was little, she had observed the ways of her mother, as well as other old people who did very bizarre things to produce the results they desired. Mother said that as a storyteller, she noted that Grandma told at least three types of stories. The first type, which Mother deemed innocent and harmless, were the common folktales which Grandma related to entertain little children. The other two types were stories Grandma told to accompany certain healing rituals. For example, there were those very long and complex narratives that took hours, even a whole day and a whole night, to recount. Since very deep and sometimes unintelligible archaic terms were used to recite or chant these stories, this type was known only to a few very old men and women at that time. The third type were stories Grandma *imagined*, and then she *made believe* that these were real stories. Mother said that Grandma was really good at imagining things and making up stories that she ingeniously and convincingly related to her patients. Once she established the story that was 'appropriate' and pleasing or soothing to her patient, the case was considered closed; she would not encourage talking about the problem or the illness again, but would act as if everything was fine, or would be fine. Because they believed in the custom, her patients would believe the 'healing story' given to them, and they would do whatever else they were instructed to do when they went home. Mother believed that the latter two types of storytelling were bizarre pagan practices with no scientific basis.

"So you imitated Apu's pagan ways?" I asked, very surprised to learn about Mother's secret.

"No, no," Mother strongly objected. "I did not know what I was doing then. It was only recently that it occurred to me that it may have actually been the same as what she had been doing!"

"And?"

"At first, I felt horrible. I was afraid I had been sinning – that I was actually no different from my heathen mother! That I may have been using the *Devil's technique*! I really thought about it a lot." She paused, and glanced at me.

I waited for her to continue.

"And I thought . . . if it was a sin . . . it was a sin that brought me closer to God. So I asked God to forgive me."

She paused again and looked out the window. A cool breeze played in and out the half-opened window.

"And then one day, I came across a verse in the Bible that gave me hope."

She opened the Bible she had been holding and pointed to an underlined verse:

Finally, brothers and sisters, whatever is true, whatever is noble, whatever is right, whatever is pure, whatever is lovely, whatever is admirable — if anything is excellent or praiseworthy — think about such things.[11]

"So I reasoned, if what I had been thinking and imagining was

---

[11] Philippians 4:8 New International Version.

not harming anyone, and if Ina's *imagination* and *storytelling* actually helped heal the sick, wouldn't that be something admirable and worthy of praise?"

Mother looked at me in a manner as if seeking my agreement with what she thought. I did not say anything. I needed more time to ruminate and understand all that she had been telling me.

"Ahhh, there are just too many confusing things in this world, my child. I advise you to pray to God for help and guidance about your future."

Mother appeared a little confused as she concluded the talk that night. She left my room, filling my head with even more things to ponder.

14

THE HAVES AND THE HAVE NOTS

After I finished secondary school, Mother traveled with me to the city. To seek advice and possibly financial assistance, she took me to the house of her 'mom', or godmother, from a long time ago, whom she had not seen for more than three decades. The matriarch was still alive, and one of her daughters, whom Mother cared for when she worked for the family, agreed to take me in and share a room with her assistant. While they agreed that Mother would still be responsible for paying my college tuition, they agreed that my board and lodging would be covered in exchange for running errands and doing some housework. They decided that I would attend the same private Catholic school where Mother had completed her secondary education. I was more than grateful that the cost of my college education would be reduced.

My fate, however, takes a different turn. Back in the province, my sister sent a telegram informing me that they had just received a letter addressed to me. It was a university admission letter with a full scholarship grant from the country's most prestigious state university. We were to learn that the offer was part of the state university's affirmative action program, which aimed to provide young indigenous people from remote rural areas equal access to study at the university, which is known for its highly competitive and stringent admission procedures. Mother and I were certainly relieved that, unexpectedly, I could go to college entirely cost-free! Although Mother was informed that the university which admitted me is the best in the country, what she was not told was that it has an equal reputation of being communist – a place for atheists, agnostics, rebels and free thinkers – the very opposite of the Catholic university that she so much cherished with nostalgia.

Mother's godmother advised that I be placed in a certain Catholic dormitory exclusively for girls. This dorm happened to be within walking distance of the college campus where I would be attending. When Mother expressed concern about the cost of living in a private Catholic dormitory, her godmother quickly assured her that the cost would certainly be affordable since the dormitory is a 'charity' institution named after the charitable St. Claire. So, Mother's godmother called St. Claire's to inquire about the dormitory and inform the management about me – a *native* and a *provinciana* – who needed a place, only to be told that the dormitory was already full and could not accommodate me. However, the matriarch proved to be quite influential in the city's Catholic circles, as after further discussions with the nuns, I was finally sent to be interviewed before being accepted into the Catholic girls' dormitory.

I was ushered into a large room with walls painted white, pink, and cream. A big, sturdy, dark-colored wooden table was at the center. A very serious-looking nun sat at the table, poring over some documents. Without looking at me, she told me to sit down. There were two chairs on both sides of her table, but I chose to sit on a chair next to the wall. When she was through with the documents she was looking at, she raised her gaze and peered over her thick reading glasses. I felt her penetrating but impersonal gaze scrutinize me, from head to toe. She asked me to sit on one of the chairs in front of her, which I did. After asking me several questions, the nun corroborated what Mother's godmother told Mother – that in accordance to the vows of their order, the dormitory is open to help *underprivileged* students like me. Then she went on to say that as long as I got along well with the other girls, she believed there would be no problem. She smiled and dismissed me.

Ironically and unexpectedly, it turned out that the dormitory fees were more expensive than the standard prices set by other lodging facilities for students at that time. Mother's godmother, however, convinced Mother that St. Claire's dormitory is safe, and she will be assured that I will be in good hands under the care and supervision of the nuns.

As I resided in the dormitory, I soon learned that most of the other residents were, in fact, coming from very *privileged* families from the lowlands. Chauffeured cars and wealthy parents came to pick up their daughters, bringing them home to their hometowns for the weekend, then driving them back to the dormitory when the weekend was over. As I noticed these things around me, I constantly wondered why I was born into my specific family, in a rural village-town that was also far removed from everything considered good and popular. I constantly thought of Mother, seeing her image doing her usual toil in the fields, and who could not afford to come to visit me.

In the dormitory, there were a few *mestizas*, or mixed-race girls, who were looked up to by the other girls as the epitome of beauty, wealth, and class – a social status admired and aspired for by the average Filipino. Many of the other girls appeared to have everything at their disposal; they were extravagant with food and negligent with their belongings. I became self-conscious as my poverty and lack of exposure to everything popular and fashionable became more pronounced. Although I could not afford a lot of things, I felt the pressure to conform to the other girls' more affluent lifestyles, just so in order for me not to appear so different from them and be left out. Moreover, I was the only Igorot, a highland indigenous person, living in the dormitory. And that was the very first time I felt different on the basis of my ethnicity.

My awareness of being different was highlighted when one of my roommates, upon learning that I am an Igorot, was genuinely surprised. She emphatically announced to everyone that it was unbelievable that I am an Igorot. When another roommate curiously asked her why, she said that it was because Igorots are ugly, very short, dark-skinned people who are rumored to have tails at their rears and who are incapable of learning. My roommate was definitely convinced of her notion of people like me. Due to miseducation and a deeply ingrained colonial mentality, first perpetrated by the Spaniards among their lowland flock when they were unable to penetrate the highlands, many people in my country came to view the Igorots as savages.

In her letters, Mother always advised me to be frugal in my spending, to be modest in my manners, and to always be kind and friendly to my roommates. She often reminded me that we were poor, and could not always afford to buy the things we needed, or do much of the other things that people with money could do. So my best recourse, according to her, would be to behave modestly in order for other people to like me, to treat me kindly, and possibly even give me some of their 'extra'. Mother's advice was, of course, based on her own experience. Her godmother liked her very much because she was meek and obedient.

In my letters to her, I expressed how it was bothering me to come to learn how it is that there are very rich and very poor people in the world. Her response was that she does not know why there are poor and rich people; she only knows that there are people born poor and people born rich, and it is either due to luck or to the unknown Will of God. She said that I should not be discouraged by what I see around me because, through 'hard work', and through God's 'mercy', even a person born poor can climb the ladder of success.

After one semester living in the dormitory, I had to bid goodbye to the nuns. It was not because I was bored with the compulsory weekly prayer meetings and hymnal singing, nor because I failed to get along well with my moneyed roommates. Even the nuns proved to be very kind and likable despite my first impression of them. The roommate who continued to look down on me with prejudice was a minor issue compared to the major issue of finances. Even the "combined powers" of Mother and her godmother could not bail me out. The dormitory fees went up after the school semester, and the situation was made worse by the sudden, unforeseen change in the terms of my scholarship package. The monthly stipend and the book allowance initially promised to indigenous scholars like me were disbursed for one semester only and then stopped. The explanation from the university administration was that the government implemented an austerity policy that significantly reduced the budget allocated for the state university. According to a new friend on campus, it was because the government was funneling more funds into the military budget while, at the same time, giant financial organizations like the International Monetary Fund and the World Bank, were putting pressures on the government to pay its debts. Whichever reason it was, I could no longer pay my dues to St. Claire's. So I had to leave.

I missed the relative comfort of St. Claire's as I settled into a small boarding room apartment with two new roommates. My new roommates were not students, but young female factory workers working in a nearby factory. While they were away working at the factory all night, our shared boarding room was quiet, allowing me to work on my academic requirements. During the daytime, when they were home to get some sleep, I was away at school.

As if by coincidence, my question about why there are poor people and rich people found a likely answer when I attended a university sit-in. A student leader spoke about the causes of social inequality, injustice, and poverty – topics that immediately caught my interest. In my very personal life at that time, I was experiencing the deprivation, discrimination, and unfairness the student leader-activist was talking about. He spoke about the limitations of our endless intellectual debates within the sheltered walls of our classrooms, and challenged us to act, and step outside what he called our small-world petty bourgeois comfort zones. He urged us to go and learn first-hand about the daily struggles of the common people. He emphasized that since we were studying at a state university – a public school sustained by the people's taxes – we had to serve the People – the taxpayers, and not the inept government.

Through my eventual membership in the leftist movement, the harsh reality of a wretched world opened up before me. I saw a hostile reality characterized by an *institutionalized* conflict between the Haves and the Have-Nots. Such a picture of exploitation, struggle, and suffering was both frightening and profoundly moving – even to someone like me, whom I considered to be already poor enough. People in my hometown are categorized as poor, but unlike in the big cities and other lowland provinces, everybody in my hometown has food to eat, clothes to wear, and a house to go home to. Even the one and only non-working village drunk did not have to go hungry as he could always go eat with relatives. Unlike the naked and scrawny children running and begging in the city streets, the naked children in my hometown are bright-eyed, healthy, and strong, adeptly running through lush mountains, climbing the stonewalled terraces, and swimming in crystal clear waters. Deep in the inner mountains, in that separate world where I come from, there were not what you would call very rich and very poor people.

Through the leftist movement, I had the chance to study the political, cultural and socioeconomic theories that offer to *systematically* and *scientifically* analyze and explain the bases, and the nature, of the exploitative, unjust, economic and political system which is causing the poverty of my country and the suffering of her people. To substantiate these theories, my comrades and I traveled to adjacent provinces to interact with and learn from impoverished cash crop vegetable farmers and gold miners. We also immersed ourselves in the city's urban poor families, who had been evicted from their lands in the provinces to make way for massive mining, large-scale cash crop plantations, and other so-called modern developments.

One person I spoke with related to me how his family was

uprooted from their ancestral domain in the countryside: One day, people from the government came and had his illiterate grandfather put his thumb marks on a piece of paper. Then the government people told him to keep the paper while the government keeps the land because the land belongs to the government. Hired laborers soon came; they fenced the land, then bulldozed it. When their community protested, soldiers came and escorted them to jail. They had a court hearing, but because of his grandfather's thumb marks on the piece of paper, they lost their land. His stunned grandfather could not believe what his thumb marks on a piece of paper could do. He thought that the government owning the land was outright ridiculous, because their forefathers of many generations had been living and caring for the land long before there was a government.

We also visited rice farmers in neighboring lowland provinces. These rice farmers do not own a piece of the land they till under the scorching tropical sun of the lowlands. The land is owned by only a handful of wealthy landowners who are also the country's elite businessmen and politicians.

The result of our 'systematic' and 'scientific' study of society is the analysis that our country is in a semi-colonial and semi-feudal state. Semi-colonial because we are not really an independent country. Indirect colonization by more powerful nations and their multinational and transnational corporations has bound us to the system of neocolonialism. Semi-feudal because, although many of our people work as assembly-line workers in foreign-owned multinational factories, the majority of our people are still agricultural workers with living conditions comparable to those of Europe's medieval serfs. So, in order to eliminate the vast disparity between the Haves and the Have-Nots, and to end an institutionalized exploitative system, my comrades and I believed in the necessity, and inevitability, of a communist revolution.

As I got more exposed to a bigger reality, my earlier very

personal but seemingly monumental problems, such as father's death, physical pain, teenage arguments, and my almost not making it to college due to a lack of money, all suddenly appeared small and selfish when confronted with much bigger and deeper issues affecting the whole of society. Completely unknown to Mother and to the rest of my family, I deeply involved myself in college activism. I thought I had finally found the purpose of my existence, which was to uphold justice and equality by fighting against injustice and inequality. I went about my newly discovered purpose with missionary zeal. My earlier brooding on the meaninglessness and emptiness of existence was duly replaced by what I believed to be a meaningful and noble purpose.

My fate, however, took yet another unexpected turn. Towards the end of my senior year in college, I applied and was awarded a scholarship grant to go to Tokyo, Japan, as an exchange student. This gave me the chance to see yet another alternative reality. Several months before that, however, Mother had fallen ill and was hospitalized. Just like Father earlier, I witnessed how her mind and body declined. She passed away half a year after I left for the student exchange program.

15

THE THIRD WORLD AND THE FIRST WORLD

The host university was situated in the midst of a large, historic, ancient, and lush forest, which was both beautiful and comfortable. The front of the main school building was a spacious grassy lawn dotted with flowering trees. This pretty lawn was where the easygoing students spent most of their time. In contrast to my home university, where most students were usually excited, agitated, or struggling about one thing or another, students at my host university appeared to be relaxing most of the time. They have enough leisure time to laze on the grass, read books, date, play frisbee, or socialize with friends. There was no student activism at all, and the reason was obvious – there didn't seem to be anything to be upset about. Every facility at the university, including the student dormitories, was built and furnished with first-class materials and technology. The people on campus were all friendly, courteous, and helpful. The overall atmosphere was one of ease, refinement, beauty, comfort, and, for me personally, quite luxurious. With my scholarship money unfailingly being deposited into my bank account each month, I never had to worry about my finances. For someone coming from a rustic village in a Third World country, such a convenient and carefree way of life in a beautiful natural setting, complemented by high technology, was almost like a taste of paradise. There were fun campus parties and colorful community festivals. People invited us to their homes and gave us presents. Foreign students like me were given complimentary tickets to watch very expensive kabuki plays and western symphony orchestra concerts – high-class entertainment that I would not have been able to afford otherwise.

Outside the cloistered campus, however, some social issues affecting Japanese society had not been completely veiled from us. Not far from my host university was a popular train track where people who wanted to commit suicide hurled their bodies into moving trains, and the number of people ending their lives in this manner was unbelievably large. School bullying is a very serious affair among schoolkids. I noticed many elderly people hobbling their way through the subways – a generation that seemed to have been left in oblivion by the busy-running majority. Hordes of men in elegant dark suits made their intimidating presence felt as they rushed and pounded the subway platforms. Smartly dressed and powerful, they may have looked in their corporate uniforms; their drawn faces and lackluster gazes, however, did not seem to indicate that they were happy being alive. There were several hundred homeless people on the riversides and in the parks, a social problem which I presumed to be applicable to countries like mine only. There were also unfriendly people who even appeared hostile for no apparent reason. I was later told by a Japanese friend that these people were afraid of people like me, foreigners, just because they feared and were suspicious of anything or anyone they knew nothing about.

After a school year of exquisite experiences in a First World country, my time was up. I had to go home. A couple of months before my time to leave for home, on a beautiful spring morning, when the cherry blossoms had just started blooming, I traveled to a nearby city to see the historic ruins of a medieval castle built on a mountain top. People whom I asked for directions instructed me to go towards the hills by following a certain small road. I followed the small road on foot for about 15 minutes. It led to the base of the mountain where there was a two-story house building and a parking lot. The place was deserted, and I did not know how to proceed. Frustrated, I was going to retrace my steps back to the main road when I caught a glimpse of movement in one of the parked cars. The person inside the car emerged as I walked towards the car. He was a tall, handsome young man my age with a confident tone in his voice that intimidated me. I asked him for directions on how to get to the castle ruins. He gave me some instructions that sounded far more complicated than I had anticipated. So I simply said, "Hai wakarimashita, arigatou gozaimashita" (Yes, I got it, thank you), and turned to walk back to the main road. I could feel his intensely perplexed gaze following me as I walked away. When I was about 15 meters away, I heard him start his car and follow me, and as he got parallel to me, he came to a halt and flung open the passenger door, saying, "Okurimasu!" (Get in, I'll take you there!) I assumed he was angry at me, as I was sure he might have only felt obligated to take me where I wanted to go. But the way he threw open the door, shouting at me to get in, made me feel compelled to do as he said. Although I had just met him, and his very formal and authoritative way of speaking scared me a little, I had the impression that he meant no harm. Sensing my tenseness, he began casually speaking to me, abruptly shifting from the formal manner in which he spoke with me earlier to a friendly, informal Japanese.

As soon as we turned the curve of the hill, we saw a big sign written in both Japanese and English. It indicated the entrance to where I wanted to go. We looked at each other. Relieved, I smiled. He was flustered. It turned out that we had a misunderstanding. He thought I wanted to go to a waterfall, which was about a 30-minute walk from the parking lot. The names of the waterfall and the castle ruins sounded similar but were written in different characters. Apparently, I mispronounced the name of the castle by not stressing a vowel.

He apologized and, following the sign, we entered the forest. As we drove up the steep hill, the road became narrower and darker because of the tall trees on both sides of the road. We again looked at each other, me with a nervous but heightened sense of adventure, and he with a reassuring glance. When we got to the top, his phone started ringing. He spoke hurriedly and vaguely to the person on the other end of the line. I surmised he was waiting for someone in the parking lot when I saw him, and now they were calling him. But then, after briefly answering a second call from apparently the same caller, he did something which I thought was odd. He switched off his cell phone!

Since he had brought me to my destination, and as I got out of his car, I expected him to drive back down the hill. I thought I would be free to roam the place as I pleased, relieved from awkwardly conversing in Japanese with a stranger. But, to my surprise, he also got out of the car and showed no sign of intending to leave. Instead, he was very eager to show me around, even though it was also his first time being in that place. After walking around the ruins and in the adjacent forest park for an hour or so, he wanted to take me on a tour around his nearby university campus. We ended up spending the whole afternoon together. He surprised me with his knowledge and appreciation of the two classic political novels about my country, written by Dr. Jose Rizal. I was very impressed by his knowledge and interest, knowing that young people his age do not normally spend their spare time reading about old political writings, especially about a small Third World country. My other Japanese friends, at that time, were purely into American pop culture. He introduced me to Buddhism, which led to deeper discussions. I spoke very limited Japanese and he spoke very limited English, but we seemed to understand each other. A week before leaving Japan, after my final exams, I called and asked him if we could meet for the last time before I left, but for a reason I could not understand, he was crying when he said he could not meet me. I believe we both fell in love with each other at first sight. I left Tokyo with a broken heart.

16

DARK NIGHT OF THE SOUL

I had not anticipated my homecoming to be equally sad. Things were no longer where I left them. Mother had died. A couple of close friends married; others moved to other places; and still others became busy with their personal lives. And now that I was finished with college, I felt I no longer belonged in the secure and familiar sanctuary of academia.

I noticed that I had changed a lot as well. Old friends from the leftist movement expected me to continue fighting the battle with them. However, the struggle for social justice and economic equality no longer has the same strong appeal as it once did. It was not because I was corrupted by the Japanese bourgeois and other friends from the First World. It was because a new perspective was formed out of witnessing and experiencing yet another different reality in a parallel world. Prior to the student exchange exposure, I saw reality only through a limited lens, seeing only the pains and problems of the Have-Nots, which I believed were the result of exploitation perpetrated by the Haves. In my naiveté, I had no idea that even the Haves – those who could afford to buy whatever they needed and desired to make themselves healthy and happy – were plagued by serious struggles of their own. Depression, fear, boredom, emptiness, anxiousness, dullness, and even survival issues were observed in the lives of those in the First World, along with other strange afflictions I could not fully comprehend. The rich, like the poor, are vulnerable to deep suffering and unhappy lives. Human suffering is a universal experience. In its various guises, it strikes at both the Haves and the Have-Nots.

After being charmed by the highly efficient, comfortable, and convenient Japanese way of life, the unexpected turbulence and disorder that greeted me upon my return to my Third World reality had been an unexpected, ironic bit of a culture shock. In my first couple of months back home, the world had literally and metaphorically turned dark. Wild tropical typhoons struck one after the other, destroying everything in their path and claiming people's lives and livelihoods. Roads were closed, and power and communication lines were down. The people who were forcibly confined and starved inside their cold and unlit homes were considered very fortunate by those whose houses were carried away by landslides and flash floods.

Alone, and once again, with no known purpose in life – a purpose that could at least keep a hurting soul motivated enough to want to keep on living – I again slipped into a dark space. "Everything is meaningless and wearisome. . . . Life is chasing after the wind." This was what the wise king in the Bible had discovered in his earnest search for the meaning of life. You are happy now, tomorrow you are sad. You laugh now, tomorrow you sob. The old life-questions which stirred through me when I was fifteen, resurfaced, demanding real, lasting answers. The wise words, "This too shall pass" (referring to the temporariness of everything), could not console me, since I could not fathom the sense of being continually harassed by, indeed, passing emotions and situations.

I was infected with the flu and was feverish. If I was not slumbering, I would sit by the window and watch how the wind savagely smashed the rain into house roofs and deep into the earth, like a million sharp arrows being hurled by an angry god in the sky. It didn't help that I kept hearing rumors that God's punishment was coming and that the end was near. The throbbing in my head felt like it wanted to compete with nature's fury, or maybe it was watching nature's fury that made it worse. In the midst of all this inner and outer turbulence, however, the debilitating pain soon began to become ironically convenient as it overpowered and silenced the noise in my head, forcing me to surrender into a state of tranquil delirium. For a couple of days, I was entertained by meaningful dreams and fantastic hallucinations, successfully diverting my attention away from the physical pain, the anguished thoughts, and the overall self-absorption.

I had a strange dream:

I just arrived home, in the village. On my way down to the kitchen, in the middle of the stairs, were two little gray mice. One of them was dead. The dead one lay on its back, its internal organs exposed. In the kitchen, I saw Sainoc standing quietly in front of the hearth; his back turned to me. I told him to catch the live mouse and rid the house of mice. Without turning to face me, he replied that he couldn't capture the alive one. "Anyway, they will grow big," he said. I told him that they would not grow big because it is in their nature to be small. I picked up the dead mouse by the tail and gave it to the cat, which was happy to toy with it. Then I asked Sainoc where Mother was. I had to ask him three times before he responded, telling me that Mother was resting in her bedroom. I went to the bedroom and saw her lying on her side; her back turned to me. I was overcome with deep longings. At that moment, all I wanted was to be with her. I was cognizant of the storm raging outside, but where she lay, looked warm, peaceful, and comfortable. I asked if I could lie down next to her. Without turning to look at me, she flatly refused. We ambiguously discussed a problem regarding the *condition* of the house, or about the mice in the house, which had annoyed me. Still, without turning to face me, she said gently, "That's why I have been telling you that we better have two separate beds". I thought to myself, 'Why the need to have separate beds when we used to sleep only in one and could still share only one?' Then we briefly talked about my other siblings. I woke up wondering what it meant for us to have 'two separate beds'.

Apart from storytelling, dream-telling was another form of

entertainment I used to share with Grandma. She encouraged me to remember my night dreams. I would relate them to her if I remembered them. In fact, seeing Grandma fly was one of my most memorable childhood night dreams. She also shared her night dreams with me; they always sounded fantastic. But there came a time when I did not care to remember my dreams and I got annoyed by her asking me about them, so I just told her I had stopped dreaming. After some months of allegedly not dreaming, and while I insisted that she relate to me the *stories and images she saw while she slept*, Grandma scolded me for being too lazy to remember my own dreams. She then told me that dreams are a way for us to understand who we are. Thus, dreams can guide us on what to do or what not to do in many important situations. She had also mentioned that through dreams, we can communicate with our ancestors and relatives on the other side.

In the above dream about Mother, it seemed apparent that I was having a *condition* – a problem I could not cope with, and so I was wanting to die – to lie down beside her and join her where she is at – where it appeared warm, peaceful, and comfortable. She refused, telling me that we better maintain 'separate beds', which perhaps meant separate worlds or dimensions.

♥ ♥ ♥

My childhood friend Mercy, who was then living and working in the city, invited me to attend their *True Believers'* worship service. To ward off my depression, I readily agreed to go with her. Mercy was delighted to tag me along; she thought it was a good chance to fix what she referred to as my unforgivable cynicism. The big rented hall was full of people. The crowd looked like a political campaign circus — as if they were trying to rally mass support for a god who is supposed to rule a kingdom high in the sky. The pastor claimed that the ruler of our world *here below* is the Devil, and, leaving all our worldly possessions behind, we have to evacuate this evil-infested world because everything awaiting us in the kingdom of God *above* has more glitter and is guaranteed to be long-lasting. The worship service lasted nearly the entire afternoon. Each member's passionate testimonies about how God had performed miracles in their lives overwhelmed me, but they didn't provide any answers to the life-questions I had hoped to find answers to by joining a gathering of Believers. Much to Mercy's chagrin, I was bored at the worship service. They appeared raucous to me. I didn't feel the same sense of awe and reverence for the divine that I usually felt when I simply sat quietly under an unassuming tree. I observed Mercy. She didn't seem to get that high while her fellow Believers were emotionally ascending higher as their charismatic preacher's fiery speech soared, inflaming every Believer's longing to reach heaven, a place where peace, happiness, contentment, and eternal wealth await them. The high level of group energy was undeniably contagious, but as the unforgivable cynic Mercy so aptly described, I managed not to get carried away. After the worship service, Mercy rushed to see her friends. She said she felt like she belonged when she was with her church people. She also confided that her network connection through her church is very advantageous for her pyramid networking side job.

17

THE ROOT OF EVIL

To this day, my former communist comrades continue to fight for the ideals of a fair, equitable society. They did not fail in their duty to remind me that if we dedicate our lives to the *struggle for mass emancipation,* if we are loyal and committed to producing a *class revolution,* we can eliminate the world's imperialists, greedy, and corrupt people. And that, as committed revolutionaries, we would be like the united workers, forging ahead on the long, arduous march to freedom – where a better, fairer, and brighter future world reality would exist.

The very wealthy owners of the *Means of Production* and their political allies already have everything. They have the money, the power, the fame, and the control. *What then drives them to want more?* My communist friend's answer to this question was simple, "Greed", he said. He maintained that those in power are simply greedy, and that in their absolute greed for more profit, power, and control, arose the root cause of the majority of the world's suffering. He said that the problem with the common people is their ignorance, and that's why there is a need to enlighten them, to politicize them, and empower them so that they can fight back against their oppressors. *But what exactly is the root of greed?* My communist friend didn't have an immediate response, but Mercy, who had been cynically listening to us, did. "The cause of greed is evilness, which is obviously caused by Satan's power," she jumped in. Mercy's remark seemed to have struck a chord with my communist friend, for he came up with his own answer. Greed, he claimed, is inherent in human nature. That is why we need laws, governments, and, yes, some form of religion to keep the 'evil nature' of man in check.

The religious believe that the Devil is the source of greed and other social ills, and that religion is the solution – that all we need to do is obey God's laws and become Christians, Muslims, or Buddhists, and we will be given the moral strength to resist the Devil's temptations. History, however, has demonstrated that in the pursuit of gold, glory, and a place in heaven in the afterlife, religion has been an instrumental ideology that exhorted people to kill and steal from one another, as well as to invade and enslave the inhabitants of other nations. The defenders of religious organizations, however, argue that it is not religion itself that drives people to do bad things. They claim that religion is simply being used by 'Devil-possessed' groups and individuals to further their greed and violent tendencies.

I found out that just like religion, politics, no matter how scientifically studied and systematically analyzed, also failed to provide a sufficient answer. The basis of Marxism – Historical Materialism – in its purely materialist approach to the study of society, may not account for *greed* as the factor that is *causing* the already wealthy owners of the Means of Production to insatiably want more. Because greed, after all, is not an empirical data or a materialist concept that can be studied using a materialist method of analysis.

Although I agree with my communist friends that it is a lofty goal to devote one's life to the forging of a fairer and better society, particularly in the defense of the oppressed, it felt to me that, beyond the systematic and scientific analysis propounded by the Historical Materialists, the fundamental cause of society's problems stems from a deeper, and most likely, an immaterial source.

So, even though I sometimes felt nostalgic for the idealism of my college days, and longed for the company of my eloquent political and intellectual friends, and although I am often moved by their self-sacrifices and the sincerity of most of them, I no longer felt the pull to stay. I set out on a different path in search of deeper answers.

18

A YOUNG URBAN PROFESSIONAL

I got a job in the city doing research and community development. Poverty alleviation was one of my long-term research interests. My job satisfied my idealistic bias, but it also left me overworked and underpaid. My daily existence was defined by a sense of scarcity and limitation. Aside from the ongoing quest to discover the meaning of life, I realized I wanted more from life itself. I wanted to read books and travel all over the world. However, such pursuits necessitate the luxury of both time and money, both of which I lacked in my circumstances.

We often hear that a wealthy man's wealth is an impediment to his spiritual growth. But there I was, working and living among the poor, seeing how a lack of money drives the poor man to scrounge for scraps, cheat, and commit crimes in order to get his hands on the little money he can. The poor man's daily struggle for survival is also a hindrance to his spiritual development. My communist comrades were right when they said, *"How can you sit still and listen to God's Words when your stomach is growling with hunger?"* But it is also true that many of the poor find solace in religion, for they *heard* it was written: *Blessed are the poor, for theirs is the kingdom of heaven.*

Although I initially assumed that I was in a better position than the presumably "less fortunate" subjects of my research and that I could help them get out of their situation, it gradually occurred to me that I didn't know any better than they did when it came to getting out of poverty, because after years of research into poverty alleviation, I failed to alleviate even myself from relative poverty. Besides being a depressive topic, reading, writing, and talking about poverty almost every single day tired and exhausted me.

Working with and for the poor taught me at least two important lessons about poverty alleviation. First, I cannot be of any more assistance to the poor, or to anyone else, if they do not help themselves. Second, I cannot help anyone if my situation isn't any better than theirs. If I myself am still 'hurting' like the proverbial wounded healer – which essentially renders me weak and too conflicted to be relied on – how could I possibly claim to heal or rescue another? In other words, if I remain poor with the poor, how could I lead the latter to a better place I know nothing about? It would be like the case of one blind leading another blind. And unfortunately, despite the mountains of books written about theories, statistics, and documented altruistic projects, it appears that no one truly knows what will genuinely and sustainably lift the poor out of poverty.

In search of a greener pasture, I changed course and set out to find my fortune in the big metropolis. I easily landed a high paying job with a multinational corporation – the antithesis of my previous job and idealistic college days. Even though my new task had little meaning for me, I was pleased with my swanky corporate job – because I was still the wide-eyed village girl who had been whisked away from her previous work environment in the stinking city slums and dusty, impoverished countryside to the 16th floor of a polished, high-rise glass building in the big city. Since my past financial history had been far from what was considered substantial, I found myself overly grateful for the sudden increase in digits in my bank account balance. And so, although I rightly deserved all the monetary yields of my labor, having been used to living in an atmosphere of lack and limitation, I found myself feeling undeserving. The effect of this perception on me was that I became complaisant towards my superiors and co-workers.

As far as financial matters were concerned, I was almost convinced that I was living a "successful life" – at least, a lifestyle that was a long way from my modest beginnings. Not until a very ordinary, yet life-altering observation occurred one day:

I was sitting at a corner table in a five-star hotel restaurant one morning, watching and observing the people eating and moving around while waiting for a business appointment. The warm morning light filtered through the massive glass walls, making the wine glasses on the tables glisten. The gentle music in the background blended well with the silent conversations and the clinking of plates and cutlery. Everything was pleasant, calm, and quiet. A few moments later, a tall, brawny, well-dressed, middle-aged man on his phone entered. My eyes followed him. At the periphery of my vision, I noticed a couple of other diners pause and stare at him as he sat in a chair one table away, directly opposite me. He had a very strong, incensed presence. He leapt to his feet and answered a phone call. The veins in his temples protruded as his face turned bright red with rage. Other diners, who appeared to be disturbed or surprised, turned to look at him. I noticed the food servers becoming tense and agitated, bumping into each other and dropping cutlery. Although he was not shouting, the man's heavily disturbed energy reverberated throughout the previously calm and intimate restaurant. After the phone call, he slumped in his chair, exhausted. He dropped his gaze to the floor. He looked like a very rich and extremely busy man. Then, suddenly, as if affected by my stare, he looked straight at me and met my gaze. He had a very painful look in his eyes. His stare was deep and intense, fearful, and terribly sad – almost as if he could cry – a cry for answers. I had goosebumps. We stared at each other, only for a brief but poignant moment. The moment was broken when my cell phone rang, and I was told that my appointment had been canceled!

I felt the midmorning heat on my skin as I stepped outside the hotel building. I walked slowly down the nicely paved sidewalk to my workplace. Cars whizzed by, and tall buildings loomed over. I felt sad and empty. I could not get the image of that anguished man out of my mind. I still had no idea what I wanted out of life, and equally had no idea what life was all about. I only came to know that I didn't want to end up like that man in the restaurant or be around people like him. He reminded me of my implacable and restless boss. He reminded me of how irritable I had become and how I had been, ironically, feeling limited and stagnant in a very fast-paced, and exciting corporate game world.

In an attempt to escape the monotony of the daily grind, I and other yuppies frequented nightspots with blaring music that prevented us from having real conversations. Despite our hectic schedules, many of us young urban professionals sought temporary refuge in loud noises—to drown out the screaming silent void inside, to distract ourselves from our various issues, to exhaust ourselves even more—so we could get some sleep and return to work for yet another day.

19

FEAR OF DEATH AND SEARCH FOR LOVE

The stranger I watched at the restaurant was, to me, a portrait of bondage – which equals suffering. He reminded me of my own fears and feelings of bondage: I was holding on to an unfulfilling job out of fear. I was afraid that if I quit my job, it would be difficult for me to find another. And if I could not find another job that paid as well as my current one, I feared slipping back into poverty. If the worst happens and I find myself jobless, especially in a country where many people do all they can to flee, where will I get the money to survive? I was told that if I did not stick to a job, I would starve, and die. It became apparent that no matter how much I overtly despised life, I covertly feared death. I felt trapped.

I found myself in a relationship where I was certainly convinced that I was in love. But when the boyfriend and I argued, we were probably worse than God and Satan. Although I had been told that sacrifices and compromises are an unavoidable consequence of being 'in love,' I seriously wondered why my sacrifices and compromises had left me angry and bitter at the end of the day. I was told that it was because my love was not unconditional.

Time and again, the boyfriend would castigate me: "Your anger is bad, and that is your problem." To treat my anger, he dragged me to his spiritual guru, who counseled me, telling me that anger is a most despicable attribute – a manifestation of the 'dark side'. And that if I want to follow a spiritual path, what he called the 'path of light', I should restrain myself from being an angry, emotional woman. I followed the guru's advice as it certainly sounded wise; but as I suppressed and hid my anger and emotions, they turned into fury, which was even harder to subdue. And for being unable to control my 'despicable anger', I was ridden with guilt, and I hated myself.

I had the expectation that my human needs to be loved and cared for would be fulfilled by being in a relationship. I showered my affections and attention on the boyfriend, assuming that he would do the same. But when the boyfriend and the relationship failed to meet my expectations, I became sad, frustrated and resentful. For expecting, or even demanding to be loved in return, it appears that my love was far from unconditional, or 'real love'. So I asked myself if I was truly in love, if I really knew what love was.

My understanding of 'love' was formed by what my high school teacher taught me in a class called Values Education. Although it was a public school, the teacher also happened to be a catechist. She taught us that there are three types of love. The first and foremost is love for God. Love for God, according to her, is at the heart of God's first three commandments of the Ten Commandments given to Moses. The second type is love for our neighbors, which is the essence of God's seventh to tenth commandments. The third type of love is self-love. The teacher avowed that there was no mention of loving oneself in God's Ten Commandments. The love for self, therefore, according to the teacher, is pure vanity – an undesirable type of love, as there is nothing in our "sinful selves" to be loved in the first place.

As a woman in a world where some men have become too insensitive to comprehend the realm of the unspoken, I did, at times, find it necessary to speak my opinions out loud. However, the boyfriend strongly objected to being spoken to out loud, for it did threaten his sense of masculinity. Gradually, I learned that in order to get what I wanted, I had to be willing to be trained to become meek and subservient; otherwise, the boyfriend would withdraw his affection. And, because I needed his love and attention, I agreed to be meek. But my meekness resulted in suppressed emotions and unspoken desires. The source of my anger, I discovered, was my learned inability to freely express my feelings and opinions.

Mother had too often advised me to be modest and humble in order for others to like me; so that others may find me agreeable, and that they may even give me their 'extra'. As a good Christian, she taught me to turn the other cheek if someone slaps me. My meekness, however, was not a result of practicing the Christian virtue of humility or of following Jesus' teachings about turning the other cheek. My meekness stemmed from a lack of self-worth. I discovered that I lacked self-worth because I lacked self-love. I did not love myself because I held on to the belief that love is to be offered to God and to others only, and that caring for or prioritizing oneself is selfish, vain, and thus sinful. Moreover, I unwittingly consented to the spiritual guru's opinion that by being an angry, emotional woman, I am not good enough.

I had been needy for the boyfriend's affection and validation. On his part, he had the need to be needed. He needed me to need him, as my need for him also validated him in a way. It soon became clear that we needed each other more than we loved each other. But the thought of breaking up with him terrified me because I was afraid of being alone. I thought I would die without him. I was afraid to die. Such was my great fear of death and my desperation to be loved that I clung on to difficult circumstances at the expense of my happiness.

I suppose there are at least two ways of perceiving oneself: either God is within oneself, and loving one's self is also loving God; or the Devil is within oneself, and one's self does not deserve to be loved. My Values Education teacher seemed to believe the latter and instilled in us youngsters that this was the truth.

20

CONFRONTING FEARS

Adding to my fatigue from work and frustrations in my relationship, I slept at night with recurring dreams of being stalked by some fearsome, obscure characters. Though I tried to ignore the feelings triggered by such dreams when I awoke in the morning, the unpleasant residue of the dream lingered for the rest of the day.

In my hometown, there are two adjacent mountains by the roadside, forming a corner at the point where they meet. Along this corner flows a narrow creek, which receives very limited sunlight. When I was a child, I would get irrationally apprehensive whenever I walked past this roadside creek, especially when it got dark in the evenings. As I got closer to the creek, I would quicken my pace and then sprint past it as fast as I could. And when I ran, something dreadful seemed to run after me, scaring me even more. Grandma's advice was that I must turn around and, without fear, speak aloud, telling the sinister spirit to 'show its face'. Grandma said that if I kept being afraid, the spirit would become bolder and scarier; if I didn't, the spirit would become afraid of me and leave me alone. She explained that this is the same technique we use when we dream of someone or something challenging or chasing us: we must stop running and turn around to look the challenger in the face. She assured me that if I behave like this when I have bad dreams, I will feel great when I wake up in the morning. If I keep running, the sinister spirit will either catch up with me or pursue me for a long time. If it catches up with me, it will ride on my back, and I will be carrying its weight wherever I go. And being chased for a long time will eventually exhaust me so that, one day, I will just wake up tired and aged.

I came to the understanding that *fears*, whether they are embodied in the unseen entities that I feared as a small child, in the troubling issues in my adult life, or in the frightful characters that appear in my dreams, must be dealt with by summoning the courage to confront them. Commanding the spooky character to 'show its face' is a way of shedding light on the issue or problem, or tracing its origins, perhaps from the shadowy depths of the unconscious, and bringing it to the light of the conscious.

In my case, I concluded that it was the absence of self-love that resulted in my lack of self-worth. In turn, the lack of self-worth, which led to my lack of self-confidence, inhibited me from self-expressing. My inability to freely express myself resulted in emotions that were contained and suppressed. These bottled up emotions led to my anger and rage. I realized that what went off course with me was that I had grown up and became a fearful, polite, consenting, stifled, less authentic *adult*.

21

IT IS ONLY A DREAM

I applied for a leave of absence from work. I told one of my less restless, non-party-going colleagues that I wanted to take a long vacation to visit my hometown, which I had not been to in a long time. With an impish smile and curiosity on his face, he asked what I would be doing on an extended trip to my hometown, since I had previously mentioned to him that it was deafeningly quiet and boring up there in the mountains. I confided to him that I had been feeling lost recently and that I needed to take some time off to empty my mind of worldly cares. He responded by raising an eyebrow as he twisted his lips into an amused smile. Then, as if he had second thoughts about what I had just said, he turned his swivel chair and looked at me with a serious demeanor. He said, "Hey, you should never, ever empty your mind. It's very dangerous. When you empty your mind, that's when the Devil finds the opportunity to sneak in, tempting you to think and do bad things".

A genuine concern was evident on his face. It was my turn to raise an eyebrow. It was an odd feeling that, after years of not hearing about the Devil, I had met him again, in an unlikely location, inside a high-rise building. Then my colleague told me that if I was feeling lost and alone, if I was having issues, I was very much welcome to join their Born Again Christian fellowship. He said I'd be able to meet a lot of nice young Christians in the group.

The long journey home was very bumpy and creaky. It took almost sixteen hours on two buses and one jeep ride. It was already dark when I arrived home. My body, which had long adopted a sedentary city life habit, was exhausted. I slept right away. I had an emotionally vivid dream:

I was in a supposedly familiar place, but it did not actually feel familiar to me. It was uncomfortably bright and glary, a dry and flat concrete street. There was not a single tree or plant on the street or what looked like concrete or paved surroundings. The street was almost deserted. There were only occasional passersby who strictly minded their own business. I was standing at what appeared to be a crossroad, not knowing what to do or where to go. The thought of Mother, who I was consciously aware of having already passed away, occurred in my mind. The thought of her reminded me of my aloneness, and I felt very sad. Then I was in a forest with many trees. I saw a small white cross suspended in the air before the many lined trees. The sight of the cross evoked an overwhelming emotion of longing for Mother. I started crying. Then I woke up and realized I had been dreaming. I found myself sitting inside a small, low-ceilinged, one-room, square house with light grayish paint. I was clueless as to whose house it was, or why I was there. The room was painted in a single color. There were no pictures or other items on the wall, and no other objects were in the room. There was only me and a small square window towards my right. I was still feeling very emotional about my dream, and my heavy feelings were compounded by my ambiguous situation in that small, blank room. So great was my sadness that any inhibitions I may have had, vanished; I howled inconsolably. Then somebody (a male voice) asked me why I was crying. I answered that I was crying because I had just had an incredibly sad dream of being alone in strange places where I did not know where to go or what to do, and when I woke up, I found myself in a desolate little box house. And then the gentle and solemn voice said, "Do not cry; *you are only dreaming*". At that point, I woke up, *again*.

As my eyes opened and focused, I recognized the familiar bedroom window in front of me. I was comforted to know that I was, in fact, at *Home* and not lost in unfamiliar places. I just had a dream within a dream: At first, I dreamt that I was at a crossroad where I did not know where to go, or what to do. Then I was in a forest where I saw a white cross that made me cry. Within that first dream, I 'awoke' to realize it was only a dream. I found myself sitting in a desolate, one-room house, and I wept some more. Then a solemn male voice asked me why I was crying. I told him that I had just woken up from a very sad dream which weighed me down. The voice then told me not to cry because I was only dreaming. Then, for the second and final time, I awoke from the second dream to find that the entire ordeal and my intense emotions had been a dream all along.

Although I felt relieved upon awakening, the heavy feelings from the double dream continued to weigh me down. It was only after I wrote down and interpreted what the dream possibly meant for me personally that I felt better. It seemed clear that the seemingly familiar, but really unfamiliar dry and concrete streets and surroundings were symbolic of where I was at that certain juncture in my life. It was the urban environment I had been living in. The crossroad represented my confused, uncertain, or ambiguous situation in which I needed to decide where I should go or what I should do with my life. Upon seeing the small white cross in the forest, the first thought that occurred to me was of my religiously devoted mother. I cried because I felt so alone without her. The small, square room (where I found myself after waking up from the first dream) could have represented my confined cubicle workplace, or it could have represented the constraint and confinement I was experiencing at the time. The voice telling me not to cry because I was only dreaming was the only uplifting aspect of that otherwise emotionally charged double dream.

Grandma used to say that the sooner we wake up from a bad dream, the better it is for our feelings. However, when we are in the midst of a dream, the feelings and events in the dream appear to be nothing but real. Thus, we have no idea that its reality is only a temporary reality from which we will soon awaken. Contemplating the above double dream, I thought that if I had been *lucid*, all I could have done to end my onerous dream was to awaken from it, so that I did not have to suffer through it by prolonging it.

22

THE CROW

I walked leisurely towards the ugwor, at the clearing in the forest. It had been many years since my last visit. Since I started working in the city, I have barely returned home. I engrossed myself in my work. At first, it was about helping the poor and researching ways to alleviate or end poverty. When I couldn't see how poverty could be alleviated in a sustainable way, I worked hard for money to enrich myself, hoping that someday I would be rich enough to have some 'extra' to give to the poor.

Lost in thoughts, I missed the trail leading up to the ugwor. The path was no longer discernible. The villagers appeared to have completely abandoned the ugwor. I had to fight my way through the intertwining vines and dense undergrowth. Thorns pricked me, and I bled. From what used to be an open, sunlit space, the clearing was now barely a clearing. Tree roots, thorny shrubs, and vines had crawled all over the place, while branches and small plants extended towards the ugwor, significantly shrinking it to the size of a small shallow pond.

I sat down at the water's edge and stared at my reflection for a long time. My reverie was interrupted by the rustling of feathers and the soft caw of a crow. From my peripheral vision, I saw the bird land on a nearby branch. I did not think much of the bird, though I had a slight afterthought that its proximity seemed to be quite unusually too close for any wild bird to go near humans. Crows were not a common sight in my hometown, and the very few that could be seen lived only in the mountains.

The soft wind and falling leaves created little ripples in the water. My reflection in the water alternately blurred and cleared. I felt chilly. I looked around and realized that a ball of mist had engulfed the area. The clouds moved in and blocked the little sunlight that was available. It was by chance that I looked up, just in time to see the crow alight from the branch and land on the ground very near me, about four meters away. I was taken aback.

The crow was totally unaffected by my bewildered reaction. Instead, with startling audacity and commanding intensity, its dark, piercing eyes looked straight at me. Intimidated, I felt compelled to just sit there. Very slowly, in what felt like an eternity, the bird started advancing towards me. When it was about one meter away, it stopped walking, but it continued to steadily hold my gaze. Overcome with dread, I was unable to move. On impulse, I thought:

"Leave me alone, or I'll run away."

"Run away . . . as you turn to go, I'll peck at your back."

The bird responded with severity, through an inescapably distinct thought that occurred in my own mind.

The totality of my awareness narrowed on the bird. Everything else faded into the background.

There was only me, and a menacing jet-black bird in front of me.

It stepped forward again and continued to approach in extremely, exaggerated slow motion. When it reached about two feet away, it again paused.

"I'll run as fast as I can," I thought in my mind.

"Try it; the tangled and thorny undergrowth will catch you like a net." The bird replied with intensity; its fierce but composed stare, unabated.

Deep inside me, I knew that the bird was right. I already felt disoriented about where I was. I could not possibly find my way easily out through the thick forest undergrowth. And obviously, if indeed it intended to peck at my back, the bird was much faster than me. I could swear that even the sporadic thoughts that went through my mind, trembled in fear.

It started to inch its way towards me again – in exceptionally slow motion. I was too terrified to move. I could not take my eyes off the bird. Perhaps I did not even blink. I feared it would attack me the moment I shifted my gaze away from it. Inexplicably, although it had been walking towards me and I could see the movements of its tiny legs as it approached, it was never able to reach me. The bird's distance of about two feet remained constant. We locked eyes for what seemed like perpetuity.

Suddenly, a flurry came and went, and with it, the crow was gone in the blink of an eye. I did not see it fly away. It was simply no longer there.

The state of suspended awareness that seemed to have overwhelmed me came to an end when I became aware of the sound of dogs barking and men talking from a distance. I could not see them, but I supposed they were villagers entering or leaving the forest. I felt greatly relieved at the presence of another human being. My numbness started to dissipate.

After a few moments, I took a cautious step towards the huge, very old tree. I sat down at the base. My hands and feet were very cold. I noticed I was a bit shaking. Interlocking my arms across my chest, I gently rocked my upper body to and fro in a desperate attempt to relax myself.

I reflected on what had just occurred. During that exchange with the mysterious bird, there was no consciousness, time, or effort to consider whether what was happening was real or if I was sleeping and dreaming. My first instinct was to flee, but the bird's compelling presence and terrifying stare had frozen me on the spot!

Memories started to pour in. I remembered a certain boy from school who used to tease me about going to this place in the forest by myself. He told me that he had heard that this locale was a dangerous place for sorcery. To further scare me, he related some of the vague village old tales about passing overnight hunters who heard some semblance of music and incessant but indistinct conversations coming from somewhere around this area. As a child, I was not unaware of these old stories, but perhaps because of Grandma and my familiarity with the place, I either disregarded the rumors, or I somehow took them as intrinsic to the forest – neither scary nor evil, but harmless and normal. I remembered that I later asked Mother if the site was truly a dangerous place of sorcery. She related that a very long time ago, under the huge old tree, to spare the crops from strong typhoons, the old folks did rituals to either mitigate the impact, or curb the direction of a disastrous typhoon. Instead of being scared, I was awed by the magic that was performed in this place. I proudly related this information to the boy, who laughed and dismissed what I said as a bunch of lies and old superstition.

In one of the family gatherings, I once heard an uncle relate a story about the good ol' days when he was a young man: he and his friends were having a bonfire outside on a moonless and starless night when, all of a sudden, a sharp beam of light shot out from the dark sky towards the direction of this ugwor in the forest. Uncle was adamant that it was not like one of those shooting stars that were commonly seen during clear nights. He said that as this forest was far from where they were having a bonfire, none of them felt interested or adventurous enough to go and investigate what the phenomenon might have been.

Mother once told me that many years ago, gold prospectors found gold in this mountain where the ugwor was. A foreign mining company wanted to extract the gold, but the people protested. Led by the elder women of the communities, half-naked village women marched towards the site to shame and drive away the all-male crew of the mining company. Mother claimed that if it were the men of the villages who went to confront the gold prospectors, violence could have immediately ensued. The topless women arrived wearing only their traditional wraparound skirts, cursing, yelling, and wailing as they uprooted and flung the mining company's tents and various implements. Meanwhile, the men of the villages were in their hiding places, ready to attack if the gold prospectors hurt any of their women.

I could only imagine the shock on the faces of the gold prospectors (who were almost certainly Christians by faith) upon encountering such angry, defiant, unashamed, scantily dressed women. That incident drove the gold diggers away without a fight – and fortunately, for good.[12]

As these memories and stories crossed my mind, I felt a pang of sadness and a deep longing for something I could not name. I think I was feeling reluctantly nostalgic. I felt like I had become a stranger in my childhood playground. It struck me as odd that this old haven of warmth, comfort, and heightened feelings of wonderment had turned cold and hostile. Dense, tangled, thorny undergrowth now abounds in the originally cleared, luminous, and sunlit forest ugwor. And since the sunlight barely reached the ground, the environs remained uncomfortably damp. An uncanny atmosphere evinced a certain wildness which I had not known before. I was pondering this transformation of the locale when it occurred to me, if I was not the one who was transformed.

---

[12] In the Igorot cultural context, when a woman deliberately exposes her private parts in anger, protest, or defiance against a man, an Igorot man knows better to look away and leave. It was believed that if a man looked at a furious naked woman who exposed her private parts in order to shame and curse him, he would be blinded and cursed. This taboo could explain why there were no cases of rape in Igorotland in the past. Although the gold prospectors and miners in the story were not Igorots, it was unclear whether they were aware of and believed in the taboo associated with the women's act.

After being away in the urban jungle for a long time, I wondered if it wasn't just my re-aligned perception that made the forest appear alien and hostile, because as I re-adjusted my thoughts about it – and as I looked again – the forest actually appeared hauntingly marvelous and mysteriously inviting, in its nebulousness, through the gathering mists. It was at this moment when it dawned on me that this locale, with its Sacred Tree and Eternal Ugwor, was a place of consecration, a natural place of worship for my ancestors, but with the absence of carved images and other paraphernalia found in churches, shrines, and temples.

The story about how the bold women chased away the gold miners put a smile on my face. I stood up, and navigating through the mesh of undergrowth, I found my way back *Home*.

23

FREEDOM

Against the protestations of friends and family for allegedly wasting my "position" and "credentials," I returned from my vacation and handed in my resignation letter to my very surprised boss.

I had been performing my corporate job for survival reasons only. Every day had been a painful contradiction. While I toiled for the preservation of my physical body, my soul was wilting away. My situation fittingly reminded me of Grandma's story about the still water of the River Kok. Like the stale and stagnant water of the River Kok, I felt like I had become stale and stagnant.

After I was formally released from my employment, as well as having the courage to break up with the boyfriend, I went home, back to the village. And for the first time since Mother died, I spent the Christmas holidays there. On the first day of the New Year, following a wish-making tradition I learned from the Japanese, I climbed a nearby hill, intending to make a wish for a new life while watching the first rays of the sun as the new year dawned. Although it was still dark, I was familiar with the trail as it was a mountain where I used to pick wild blueberries as a child. As I was climbing up the mountain, however, the peace of mind I had hoped to obtain by quitting my job was not happening. An intense, tumultuous dialogue raged in my head as conflicting trains of thoughts debated the sanity of my sudden decision to drop everything – my career's upward trajectory, my source of income, my relationships – without any idea of what I was going to do next. Upon reaching the top of the mountain, at the height of my anxiety, I looked up at the brightening sky, and, just as Mother had done before, I called out loud to God:

"Enough! I refuse to perform this bloody pointless toil just to sustain this bloody meaningless life!"

I certainly was not expecting a prompt response from God. I just wanted to vent out my inner torment. But to my astonishment, "God" responded right there and then:

"Sure, child, you are free. You have the freedom to choose, remember?"

'God' spoke through a similarly loud, thunderous thought seemingly emanating from my own mind, which frightened me. The first 'rational' thought that occurred to me was that either my exhausted mind was playing tricks on me, or that the mischievous *adi kaila*[13] who live in those mountains were taunting me. I was considering who might have responded to me when I thought I heard stifled laughter. I paused. I looked behind me, around me. I listened intently. Nothing. There was nothing unusually audible besides the normal sounds of the woodland. But whenever my mind started to dialogue, I seemed to hear a soft chuckle, and whenever I stopped to listen, the laughter disappeared.

Then it occurred to me that it was possible that my disregard of traditional mountain-going protocols, against making unnecessary loud noises, might have disturbed, and then inspired some unseen beings to get back at me. My hair stood on end; I felt a chill run down my spine. Totally forgetting my New Year's agenda to make a wish, I scurried down the mountain and almost tumbled down as I bumped into a couple of very surprised goats, one black-spotted and the other, white-spotted.

---

[13] Invisibles, or unseen beings or spirits.

24

THE CURSE OF GOD

A great philosopher once said, "An unexamined life is not worth living." I thought it was indeed absurd and *irrational* to continue spending my life pulling and pushing to obtain more 'sacks of rice' so that I could keep living, even though I had no idea why I should keep on living in the first place. Just like other seekers, I had sought out a guru – someone who could serve as a spiritual guide and provide answers to my questions.

When asked why we are here and what explains our sufferings and struggles, a guru of a certain Hindu-based religious organization explained that, as a consequence of past negative karma, a soul incarnates into material existence. He claimed that our current sufferings and struggles are the outcome of our wrongdoings in the past. According to the guru, it is actually *undesirable* to be born on earth, which is the sphere of gross matter. He said that existing in a material body entails vulnerability to diseases, pain, hard labor, and other such afflictions that prey on souls that occupy physical bodies. Having a physical or material existence, therefore, is a sort of *punishment*. The guru professed that a *cyclical* pattern of karma and reincarnation in the sphere of gross matter characterizes humankind's doomed existence, not until we find a *way out* of the cycle through a process called *enlightenment*. The fastest way out (a path to enlightenment), according to the guru, is through devotional service to God, which is observed by strictly adhering to certain practices that are deemed good and moral, while avoiding certain other practices that are deemed immoral, impure, and worldly. The regular chanting of God's holy names is imperative in this type of devotional service.

I was initially drawn to this Hindu-based religious organization as it appeared exotic and different from the Christian tradition I was raised in. However, I soon discovered a striking parallel between the aforementioned teachings and Catholicism's teachings on Original Sin and the Fall of Man. Based on Christian lore, Adam and Eve did not have to 'work for a living' or 'earn their living' while in the Garden of Eden. They simply picked and ate the fruits of the plants and trees abundantly provided by God. I imagined that perhaps they spent most of their time pleasantly roaming and idling around, possibly lazing on soft grass under the shade of a robust flowering fruit tree, sharing their thoughts, marveling at the mystery and loveliness of their naked bodies, and basking in the beauty and abundance that was all around them. The above picture is my idea of what a really good life is – if only I did not have to be somewhere else doing something else "to earn my right to exist". According to the Catholic version of the story, when Adam and Eve disobeyed God and committed the Original Sin, God expelled them from paradise as a punishment for their transgression.

It does appear that God was truly offended by the acts of Adam and Eve; that He had to curse the earth, condemn the first man and woman and all their future generations to a lifetime of painful toil. God uttered a powerful incantation that forever denied humankind from living a life of ease and abundance in paradise:

"Cursed is the ground because of you!

through painful toil you will eat of it

all the days of your life!

It will produce thorns and thistles for you,

and you will eat the plants of the field.

By the sweat of your brow you will eat your food

until you return to the ground,

since from it you were taken;

for dust you are!

and to dust you will return!"[14]

True to His word, it does feel that God's curse has never been lifted from humanity since the Fall of Man. I watched how family, friends, and most other people struggled day in and day out just to get by for another day or two. For not having yet returned to the dust from which we had been taken, it does appear that not until we die, there is no end to the mandatory labor we have been sentenced to. The world does indeed resemble a depressing labor camp.

To me, the concept of 'working in order to live' is absurd and an oxymoron. If life on Earth is a 'punishment', and thus an unfavorable state of being, then the enduring tradition of working to live ironically perpetuates this unfavorable state of punishment.

It's perplexing why an all-loving Father God created humankind and was always ready to spank His "little children" whenever they proved to be weak in the face of the numerous temptations He placed all around them. If I have to constantly strive to maintain a righteous demeanor in order to avoid being judged a sinner, and if I am constantly prodded to toil in order to earn my right to live, then this so-called "life" – the time between my birth and death – is not what I would call *life*.

---

[14] New International Version, Genesis 3:17-19. (Author's emphasis)

25

IMAGINED CONVERSATIONS

During the period following my joblessness, I became more and more of a cynic. With nothing much else to occupy myself with but to ponder over this burdensome Curse of God and the absurdity of life, it occurred to me that, more urgent than my concern for physical survival, I was suffering from a persistent, incurable disease, which, at times, had pushed me to the brink of death. I called this illness pathological pessimism. Euthanasia, or mercy killing, appeared to be the rational solution to my problem. For it would be in showing mercy to myself that my incurable pathological pessimism would finally see its end. Death would release me from the Curse of God, as my material body would finally return to become the inanimate dust from which it was formed. The fear of death, nonetheless, daunted me from mercy killing myself because death, like God, is a *great unknown* that does not guarantee anything.

When I was not slumbering, I spent long hours sitting on the balcony, looking out to the river in my hometown. Each time I sat there by myself, I imagined Grandma telling me more stories about the River's Journey.

"On its journey, the river undergoes many experiences and changes. It even changes its color and size. Here in our village, the color is usually crystal and shiny, reflecting the sun's radiance. But depending on the life around it, a river may turn into other colors.

"In the olden times, when we did not have mirrors on our walls, we went to the streams and rivers to look at our reflections. The river is our mirror. As we are alive, breathing, and moving, the river is also alive, breathing, and moving. If you poison the river, you will be poisoned in return. The river, like the healthy blood flowing through our veins, is the earth's blood, and as long as it is healthy and keeps flowing, all life on Earth is nourished.

"The river may grow big and may also shrink. It may unite with other rivers coming from different directions. If two or more rivers find common ground, they join together to form a larger and more powerful river. Joined rivers travel for a while, sometimes longer, sometimes shorter, sometimes forever. Often, after traveling together, joined rivers separate and go in different directions. But they would no longer be the same as when they first met, for they would have already given and taken something from each other. It's the same in a family or between friends.

"You find a friend with whom you can share your life's journey. You and your friend walk some distance, and you give and take, share, and learn from each other. But a time may come when you may have to go your separate ways. When this moment comes, you will no longer be the same people you were when you first met, for you will have added to each other's experience in the journey.

"Maybe you have to part ways because you have different opinions on how to travel downstream. Perhaps your friend wants to explore more of the nooks and crannies of the big towns while you prefer to flow along the more leisurely riverbeds of the countryside. You had a father, a mother, sisters, brothers, and me. Some of us leave first. You continue the journey with your siblings, but as you are all grown up, you feel drawn to explore different directions. Despite this, as the one big family that we are, we will all eventually be reunited at our final destination – the big ocean.

"And when in your journey, you find yourself confused and agitated, or in a turbulent mood, as if your emotions are like the river rapids – in a rough flow, so to speak – do not resist where the current takes you next. Do not be discouraged or disturbed by the ever-changing landscape. Is the river intimidated and sees itself as a victim when a massive boulder blocks its path? No, the river simply curves around the obstacle and continues to flow. Does the river tremble in fear when it finds itself standing at the edge of a precipice? Certainly not. The river makes a daring leap of faith. It is then that the murmuring river becomes a mighty, roaring waterfall! It survives the leap and discovers more of itself, its abilities and possibilities. The river knows that after a rough flow, a smooth flow is just around the bend. And when there isn't much going on and the river is flowing quietly, does it complain of boredom? Again, no. The river appreciates quiet moments as opportunities for clarity and reflection.

"So you see? The river yields, and yet it is invincible. The river can tap into its ancient spirit's wisdom and know that this is true."

"The river's spirit is ancient?" I suddenly reacted.

"Yes, the water is as old as the earth. And as a way of talking, we can say that some rivers are quite old, having been flowing on the surface of the earth for a very long time. Yet we may also speak of rivers that are newly fashioned. An *old river* has already refined and smoothed many jutting rocks and rough stones; so those parts of it coming later may follow the same path without wounding themselves too much."

I sensed Grandma's presence and wisdom as I channeled more of her river's story in these imagined conversations. I felt greatly relieved from my illness of pathological pessimism.

26

WHY IS THE RIVER FLOWING?

Still, I couldn't make a breakthrough and get an answer to my most important question: *Why is the River Flowing*? If Mother were to answer, I believe she would say, 'It is the Will of God.'

It is my utmost desire to know the Will of God.

Beginning from incipient villages, developing into towns, burgeoning into vibrant cities, bursting forth as powerful empires and great civilizations, are complex human structures and organizations that first sprang from where humble rivers flow. However, only very few among the human race pause by the river and wonder why it is flowing. And those few philosophers are labeled as mad by the rest who consider asking such a question and listening to the river murmur its answer, a waste of time.

I had asked Grandma where the river comes from and where it goes: where it begins and where it ends. She told me it comes from the sky and goes to the big ocean. I learned from my science class in school that the water in the ocean evaporates, condenses into tiny drops of water that form clouds, and then falls back to earth again as rain. It is a cycle that goes on and on and on.

What is the point of this endless cycle of motion and existence?

As Grandma put it, and as intimated in the previous dream, like our temporary dream adventures that dissipate as soon as we wake up from sleep, our experiences in life are also only *temporary realities*. The moment we become aware of the fleeting nature of our life experiences, we realize that life itself is also just a dream.

But if we are merely in the temporary act of dreaming equally temporary dreams, what is the purpose of the temporary act of dreaming an equally temporary dream? What could be the reason for the river's entire process of journeying to the sea, only to repeat the same cycle over and over – for an unknown eternity?

27

REDEMPTION

"We are God's creations, and we are created in His own image; that's who we are," said the lady who goes around people's houses clutching a Bible. I had heard about her coming to town, but the first time I met her was when she knocked at my door one rainy afternoon.

"Nabiruk yun ni Apu Hesus, apu?" (Have you found the Lord Jesus yet?) She began with that classic missionary greeting. "Apay maaw-awan, apu?" (Why is He lost?) I mumbled an equally banal response. I was relieved she did not hear me mumble, as I needed someone to chat with to divert my attention away from my morbid thoughts. As she extended her hand to shake mine, she introduced herself as Divina, but said that I may call her 'Sister Divine', as that is what she is used to being called by others.

After the introductions and some small talk about the frequent raining in my hometown, she read to me some passages from the Bible which she subsequently explained. And then she asked me if I had any questions.

I told her that I had no questions about the specific passages she had just read, but that when she knocked on the door, I had been contemplating the nature of rivers. Hesitatingly, I asked why she thought the river was flowing. She was quiet for a moment, as though considering my question. When I realized the absurdity of asking her such an odd question, I was ready to retract my inquiry and be told yet again that my question was nonsensical and simply invalid. But, I reasoned, she could always claim that the river is flowing because it is being moved by God, the so-called First

Mover. If that were her response, I'd ask her what could be urging God to move the river. When she finally spoke, however, her answer was surprisingly leaning towards the scientific. The river flowing, she said, could be properly explained in scientific terms, but since she was not a scientist, that concern did not fall under her area of expertise.

I hastily endeavored to change the topic. I asked Sister Divine why God created the Devil.

"The way out of this evil and troubled world is simple yet difficult for the majority to undertake." Sister Divine answered. "All you need to do for your salvation is to repent and acknowledge that Jesus Christ's life and blood were sacrificed to atone for your sins. You must accept that Jesus is your only hope and savior."

"I suppose I have no problem with Jesus, the holy man, but..."

"No, no, no!" she exclaimed, interrupting me in the middle of a sentence. "Jesus is not a human being! Jesus is God! He is God the Father's only Son. There is a group of Christians who are teaching that Jesus was a mere man. These people will never make it to heaven!" She stated, unequivocally.

I then asked her what would happen to Hindus, Buddhists, Muslims, Japanese, pagans, and communists. After a brief pause to consider my question, Sister Divine replied that Jesus is coming very soon, and if these *non-believers* do not repent and accept Him as their God and only savior, they will be sorry.

"Is your way the only way?" I asked.

She hesitated for a moment, as if to think. Then, while nodding, she said, "Yes, it's the only way. The Bible contains all the information we require. The *truth* is stated in the Bible: Jesus is the way, the truth, and the life. Nobody goes to the Father in heaven except through Him. Those who do not heed the Words of God as written in the Bible, shall perish."

She pronounced the last two words with an authoritative and victorious tone. Her eyes were as fervent as the sound of her voice. She went on to say that, in today's world of widespread modern communication systems, pagans can no longer make use of their ignorance as an excuse to avoid knowing and obeying God's Word.

"But my pagan ancestors sacrificed chicken blood. Worse, the Christians sacrificed their God's blood to appease the Father God. If my grandma knew the real story about Jesus, I'm sure she'd be horrified and think my mother was deranged for converting to Christianity."

Sister Divine stared at me in bewilderment. She cleared her throat. She said her throat was dry and asked if she could drink some water. I went to the kitchen and brought her a glass of water. She drank half of it. Then she said, "You do not know what you are saying, my sister. How dare you compare Jesus to a chicken? A chicken does not have a soul!"

I sincerely apologized, but as casually as I could. She gulped down the rest of the water in the glass. I asked if she wanted more. She answered no. She opened her Bible and searched for something. She read me a verse:

"The *fear* of the Lord is the beginning of knowledge, but fools despise wisdom and discipline."[15] She looked at me, then added, "Have fear, my sister . . . have fear".

"But why would God punish me, if I am His beloved child?" I asked.

"Just like I would punish my children, to set them straight, if they were misbehaving," she replied.

---

[15] Proverbs 1:7 New International Version.

Sensing that I was not satisfied with her answer, she expounded:

"We owe our lives to God, but we keep on sinning against Him, and that's why we deserve to be punished. God needs to discipline us to set us on the right path, because we do not know what we are doing."

She threw me a furtive glance and watched my reaction. I remained silent. I was having a difficult time getting my mind around the way she compared God's love to parenting.

"There is not a single soul here on earth that has not sinned. Are you willing to admit that you are a sinner?" She probed me with her very serious eyes. I felt awkward.

"Yes I do," I said.

"Good," she said.

I pointed towards Mother's image of the Virgin Mary.

"Will God punish me for placing a sunflower in front of that graven image?"

"Absolutely," she said, "the first, second, and third commandments of God order us not to..." She opened her Bible and read aloud to me the passage where God commanded us to worship only Him.

"But my late mother was fond of the blessed Virgin Mother of God." I expressed my displeasure.

She extended her hand to touch my shoulder. She peered into my eyes and said, "The Catholics are wrong, my sister, they are very wrong". She waited to see my reaction. I said nothing.

"I give you a good example," she continued after a brief pause, "if you were married, wouldn't you want your husband to love you only, apart from other women?" I agreed with a nod. She appeared to be pleased.

"It's the same with God. The *true* Believers from the *true* Church of God are referred to in the Bible as the Bride of Jesus Christ. The Bridegroom, Jesus Christ, desires that we serve Him only in worship and that we be the faithful and devoted Bride. This is according to the Bible, and you can read it for yourself," she said, her piercing gaze fixed on me. "The others are not gods: that fat Buddha, Mary, and the Pope are not gods," she added, shaking her head slowly from side to side.

She patted my back as she advised me that, for my own salvation, I should strive to be a God-fearing person.

I reflected on her admonition. It's always been a puzzle to me what 'God-fearing' entails. I kept hearing people around me proclaiming that they were God-fearing this and God-fearing that. Using God as their witness, they claim that they cannot commit such and such an 'immoral' act because they are God-fearing people. People's motivation to be kind to their neighbor appears to be driven by their fear of God's wrath rather than by their own desire to obey God's commandment to love their neighbor as they love themselves.

We noticed that the rain had stopped outside. Sister Divine stayed for about an hour. Before leaving, she instructed me to close my eyes and bow my head down for the final prayer. Leading the prayer, she asked me to repeat it aloud after her. The content of the prayer was about my admission of guilt. My acknowledgment that due to my sins, I had long been sentenced to death, but because of the intervention of Jesus Christ, who was sacrificed to pay for my sins, I was now saved. Parroting Sister Divine, as she said I should, the prayer was concluded as I pronounced my full repentance, and acceptance, that Jesus Christ is my God, and personal savior.

Then, triumphantly, Sister Divine declared to me that I had been redeemed: that my dark and heavy burden of sin had been lifted, and that it was now my duty to go forth and spread the 'good news' to non-Christians. And similar to what she had just accomplished on my behalf, Sister Divine urged me to convince the Unbelievers to repent, and accept Jesus as their only hope and savior. As an incentive, she promised that the more souls I bring into the camp of Jesus, the more blessings I will reap, and like all other redeemed sinners, I will be sitting at the right hand of the Father when the time of Judgment comes.

Since Jesus was coming very soon, Sister Divine had such an urgency to accomplish her work of saving as many souls as she could. Musing about it after she had left, I thought that perhaps her fervor to redeem people came from a sense of personal mission similar to the savior syndrome that had once possessed me as a student activist. As I had once been driven by a missionary zeal to liberate humankind from the evil clutches of capitalism and imperialism, Sister Divine was as zealous to save humankind from the evilness and ignorance of this world. Maybe the only difference between me, then, and Sister Divine, now, was that she blamed the Devil for human suffering, while I blamed politics.

That auspicious day, when Sister Divine visited me, was the day I was "redeemed".

28

THE NATURE OF GOD

When I was younger, Mother first introduced God to me as a merciful, helpful, and loving God, albeit sometimes inconsistent. As I grew older, my interest in both history and storytelling inspired me to read the Bible on my own, without Mother's intervention or personal interpretations. I was particularly fascinated by the stories in The Old Testament – an interesting account of certain tribes of people living in a specific area at a specific time in human history. Based on what I read, the temperament that God exhibited was contrary to Mother's rather sugarcoated portrayal of God. God was described in the Old Testament as jealous, insecure, autocratic, angry, manipulative, retributive, and punitive. Sister Divine's reference to the nature of God seemed to confirm the Old Testament's depiction of a terroristic God. Based on Sister Divine's narrative, it does seem that besides being wrathful and punitive, God is also attention and love deficit – much like a jealous, insecure, and possessive lover, husband, or parent indeed.

Buddhism espouses the idea that our goal is to attain Nirvana by reaching *enlightenment*. And I suppose that once enlightened, one will comprehend the Will of God. The enlightened Buddha did not, however, discuss much of his findings regarding the nature of God. They say this is because the Buddha addressed more pressing and relevant matters rather than engaging in the never-ending debate over the nature of God. And, depending on which faction of Hinduism, Buddhism, Islam, or Christianity one belongs to, there are various contentions ranging from the most basic to the most complex about who God is and why He created. Many of these religious sects and organizations find it agonizingly difficult to agree with one another, as each group insists on the absoluteness of its exclusive description, or definition of 'God'.

There are deeply religious people, such as my good friend Mercy, who do not dare ask questions because doing so implies a lack of faith in God, which only confirms one's sinfulness. There are those who go as far as to condemn art and entertainment, for they consider these sinful acts. For example, an artist creating a beautiful painting or a sculptor sculpting a human figure is perceived to be competing with God's art, as seen in the beauty of His natural creations. It is ironic that music, dance, and other forms of art and entertainment – the very things that inspire, delight, and uplift the human soul, adding some spark of joy to our otherwise somber world of wearisome toil – are condemned and frowned upon by some of the most "godly" people. It could only be an extremely jealous and insecure God who would want to stifle His people's unlimited artistic expression.

Or, contrary to what we have been told, could it be that, as some dead philosophers had postulated, we were the ones who created God, and we created Him in our own image? That is to say, do we see God as punitive, jealous, and insecure, based on how we know or perceive ourselves?

But if God did indeed create us, why did He do so? If it was us who created Him, did we do so in order to render some meaning to our existence? Did we create God out of our need to have somebody or something to believe in? To have some comforting idea to hold onto? Is it God, or is it us, who created the Devil so that we have someone to blame when things go wrong?

Who created who?

It has been my observation that the mortal human – he who declares himself to be the representative, follower, slave, or servant of God on earth – is the one who takes great offense when he hears a word that differs from his accepted notion of God. This makes one wonder if the immortal God of the mortal human requires the mortal human's defense. My childhood friend, Mercy, asked me why I had to ask the heretical questions I liked to ask. Once, while having refreshments in a café in the city, she surprised me with what I thought was a departure from our usual topic of boys and fashion styles, when she abruptly asked, "Why do you lack faith, and why don't you fear God?"

"God? Who exactly is She?" I asked dramatically in English, trying to make light of the unexpected topic she brought up.[16]

"God is a 'He', idiot!" Mercy exclaimed in English.

"We are not sure of that!" I snapped.

"It's written in the Bible! Are you your illiterate apu?" She snapped back, crossing her legs and folding her arms.

"The fear of God and the fear of death have a common denominator: the fear of the unknown," I said.

She remained quiet as she looked daggers at me in a mocking manner.

"Okay," she finally said after the pause, "but why do you take this God thing so personally and seriously, as if God especially did something very wrong to you?"

"You are right!" I exclaimed, amused, and with a sense of realization. "God twisted a vein in my brain a little more than normal, and then He allowed me to be born that way."

"And for what? To make you special?" Mercy said, with a raised eyebrow.

"For experimentation purposes only," I responded. Mercy burst

---

[16] In our language, there is no term differentiating 'he' and 'she'.

out laughing.

"And why did God choose you?"

"I am only a random sample. He could have chosen you."

"I would have refused."

"That would have made you disobedient to the Will of God, and you would have been excommunicated."

"I don't think that that is God's Will. I'm not fatalistic like you, you know . . . ," she said, amused.

"So you're saying it is the Devil's Will that I'm like me? A flawed human being?" I asked, feigning surprise.

"Obviously," she said matter-of-factly.

With pursed lips and an unimpressed askance stare at each other, we both remained silent.

I broke the stalemate: "I take this God thing seriously because I want to know about this guy who is playing God to me."

"You irritate me." Mercy responded as she rolled her eyes and took a sip of her mango juice.

"What about you, Mercedes? Don't you care at all to have a closer peek at your God's face?" I asked.

"God is a mystery," she said, echoing her preacher's words.

"Only your preacher would forbid you from investigating mysteries, so they could continue to enchant your gullible wits."

"God is God! He can do whatever He wants and to whomever He wants; that is precisely why He is God!" Mercy responded defensively, in a manner indicating she wanted to change the topic.

"That's your God, not mine!" I retorted.

She gave me a long sideways look, her lips forming a faint cynical smile as she fluttered her eyelashes.

Although I had already informed her that I was a redeemed sinner through the intercession of Sister Divine, Mercy stubbornly feared what she called 'the dark destiny of my soul'. She said that I did not sound like a redeemed sinner at all. Besides, she claimed that Sister Divine's simplistic method was highly questionable anyway. She sipped her mango juice and started eating her piece of cake, and, to my relief, we went back to talking about boys and appraising the fashion styles of those passing by on the street in front of the café.

Mercy and I can be viciously frank with each other, especially when it comes to our differing religious opinions. Ironically, our bluntness towards each other helped keep our friendship intact and interesting. We both enjoyed the comfort of having unpretentious company. When we are together, we are again free to be the unaffected village children that we once were.

29

THE PRE-CHRISTIAN IGOROT GOD

There was a time when the pagan Igorot lived in the *here and now* and had direct access to spirits and a ubiquitous presence he called 'God.' He was unaware of the Christian concepts of heaven and hell, reward and punishment in the afterlife. Then the Christians arrived and told him a *new story*: that all the spirits of nature and the dead ancestors he revered were evil. And that the Igorot, therefore, was a sinner in need of salvation. He was induced to submit and to believe only in the one true God – who also happens to be the God of those who intend to rule over him. And this God is represented by a hierarchy of priests who must now intervene and interpret for him the Will of God. He was told to give up his land as an *offering* for the building of a brick-and-mortar house of God and His representatives. Then he was taught to look forward to his reward in the afterlife – in heaven. When he refused to relinquish his land, it was forcibly taken away from him – in the name of God.

The pre-Christian Igorot concept of God is vague and varied among the Igorot ethnolinguistic groups in the Cordillera Central mountains of Luzon. For some of these groups, God, or the supreme deity, is impersonal, while for others, this impersonal deity is either combined, muddled, or confused with the identity of a 'god' who descended from the skies, married a mortal, and sired children from whom a number of Igorot groups trace their ancestral lineage. This immortal god, *Lumawig*, was described to have possessed superhuman abilities that had to be rigorously tested by mortal humans before they could allow him to marry one of their own. According to oral traditions, he stayed on Earth for a period of time but had to return to the skies where he came from; and from the skies, he watches over his human progeny. A few other Igorot ethnic groups trace their ancestry to other gods and goddesses who once walked the earth and lived among them, such as *Bugan* and *Wigan* – female and male deities from the skies.

My tribe or ethnic group did not have a Lumawig god-story, nor did we have Bugan and Wigan goddess-and-god-parents. But, like the other Igorot groups, there is an acknowledgement of a supreme deity who, in essence, is felt as a presence: an omnipresent *observer*, a force greater and beyond the usual and ordinary thinking and preoccupations of the people, yet at the same time, innately understood to permeate every creation. This great presence is impersonal, with no known gender or descriptions. In contrast to the much talked about Christian God, my people's pre-Christian notion of the supreme deity was generally unexpressed and unarticulated. Perhaps because they deemed it impractical to put into words what they felt was beyond their ability to express. On occasions where there may be a need to refer to this great presence, roughly translated into English, the term used to refer to *It* is, 'The Onlooker'[17]. When you listen to the stories of the elders, you will notice that they rarely mention God. Instead, they talk about our ancestors – their feats and exploits; how they lived their lives on Earth, and how they handled life's challenges. Their non-preoccupation with an abstract supreme deity can also be gleaned from their daily rituals. For example, when they are out in the fields or in the forests, before they eat their meal, they pray and offer a small portion of their food, not necessarily to a god above, but to the nature spirits around them, to their ancestral spirits, whom they believe are always with them, and they pour a little of their native liquor on the earth – for the earth to partake of the drink and yield them bountiful harvests and fat animals.

Although the various Igorot groups and subgroups may not have a clear definition and description of what they call their 'God',

---

[17] *Omay-ayong.*

what is certainly common among them is the belief in the existence of spirit beings that abound all around them. Nature spirits, ancestral spirits, and celestial spirits are examples of these. They are collectively referred to as the adi kaila – the 'invisibles' or the 'unseen'. While the people did not actively bother with The Great Onlooker, they dealt with the many spirit beings, or 'spirit forces' whom they believed had an immediate relationship and effect on their day-to-day lives. These spirit forces are *neutral*, but depending on one's relationship or interaction with them, they can become malevolent or benevolent.

Contrary to popular notion, the people are not necessarily at the mercy of these unseen malevolent and benevolent forces, or spirit beings. Nonetheless, it is common for ordinary village folk to perceive themselves as subject to these invisible forces, such as when they are overwhelmed by situations over which they believe they have no control. But as far as the shaman, the sorcerer, the native priest, or other knowledgeable individuals are concerned, through rituals and prayers, these spirit forces can be moved or manipulated to bring about desired results. The shamans and sorcerers resort to bribing, coaxing, appeasing, and even threatening the spirit beings in order for the latter to assist the former in achieving certain goals. As a result, the layperson seeks the assistance of such shamans and sorcerers to mediate and negotiate between himself and the spirit beings of the unseen realms.

So, different from the Christian concept of God, whose nature and personality are presumably known as references and descriptions of 'Him' are inscribed in inviolable holy books, the pre-Christian Igorot God, whose traits and identity are not inscribed in any sacred text or stone, is devoid of absolute definitions. Thus, having no defined temperament or biases assigned to the pre-Christian Igorot God, no single tribe or ethnic group can insist on their opinions of God, nor can any group claim to be God's chosen people favored over the other groups.

It would seem that the mortal human's insistence on defining an immortal God, in human terms, is born of humans' insecurity or a lack of faith. Humans are not at ease with a God who is nebulous, ambiguous, and indefinable. They needed a concrete, tangible image of God, which they then carved or drew in the *likeness of man* to remind them of God's presence. Meanwhile, the animistic Igorot, whom Christians scorned for not having a concrete image to worship or a walled church to worship in, revered and freely worshiped all of nature, where he intuitively felt God's presence.

Consistently depicting God in a specific image, in my opinion, gradually limited our imagination and our opinion of an otherwise limitless God. Worshipping exclusively within walled churches and temples also created walls, divisions, and tunnel visions among us. For some cultures, building fixed and solid 'houses of God' is a mark of advanced civilization, as these material structures are perceived as empirical evidence, a measure of humanity's progress and evolution. This is in stark contrast to the natural, fluid, and elusive world of *The Indigenous*. Even though they may have been built by laboring slaves under the orders of tyrants or pompous high priests who ordered the construction of intimidating structures and imposing monuments, primarily to showcase the extent of their influence and power, there is no doubt that these monumental structures are divinely inspired great works of art, expressing man's creativity and sophistication. However, regardless of the grandiosity of these concrete houses of worship, as with any other material representations of the immaterial, people's attention has been diverted away from the eternal toward the temporal. Most people now identify primarily with the material, the visible, and the limited, alienating themselves from the invisible and eternal spirit realms from which life, or animation, emanates from.

The Indigenous have a different perspective on *reality*. For them, life on the physical earth plane is transitory. This way of seeing explains the evanescent and ethereal civilizations that characterize nonintrusive indigenous cultures. Indigenous peoples have walked the earth for the longest time, but they lacked the cleverness to build boxlike worship structures 'to house' their God, with whom they could then make appointments on Sundays. The Indigenous God appears to be too big and too diffuse to be contained within the confines of space and time. There was also no need for dictatorial books or doctrinaire sutras to record and thus rigidify and limit the stories of the unbounded, pre-Christian Igorot God.

30

SOUL CAPTURE

An 'imagination captured' by a particular *hegemonic story* sourced from the outside is tantamount to a 'captured soul'. A *story sourced from the external* is a story that is not born out of an individual's, or a group's *experiential* search for truth. It is a story that is not rooted in and drawn from the heart of a people's distinct culture and history. And it is usually a story aggressively disseminated and promoted by those who have something to gain from its propagation. According to the elders in the village, in the practice of sorcery, a person whose soul is captured and trapped will become ill. She forgets who she is, loses her consciousness, and becomes subject to the sorcerer's will – until the spell is undone, or she dies.

This is the case of the *Philip*pine people, who are confused about their identity, and yet are unaware of their confusion. To begin with, they proudly bear the name of the one who invaded and enslaved them: King *Philip* II of Spain. In presenting their culture and heritage to the rest of the world, absurd as it is, they are overly proud to showcase the very symbol of their enslavement – their dense, dark, and stocky colonial churches. Their favored archetypal symbol, a common sight in all Catholic churches across the country, is the morbid image of the Crucified Christ, made even more dramatic by the depiction of blood dripping from His so-called Five Holy Wounds. It is no wonder why the *Philip*pino masses place such a high moral and spiritual value on suffering and martyrdom; an attribute that may have contributed to their *culture of servitude*, for which they are known around the world. At the same time, they look for a champion in a tough-talking politician or in a charismatic messianic preacher in whom they place their full faith to rescue them from their life's troubles. During Holy Week, an important observance for the faithful, they parade through the streets, displaying impressive blood-filled acts of self-flagellation and even literal crucifixion. It seems that somebody has told the Believer that in order to be worthy in the eyes of God, one has to prove it to God by wounding oneself; and it has to be in public so that everybody else may witness and commiserate on the moral and spiritual value of passionate suffering, as exemplified by the crucified Son of God. And, as they embraced the colonizer's religion and ethos, they also inherited its centuries-old scourge: the crusade against the Moors, a medieval battle which continues to play out in the *Philip*pines' southern islands. And when it comes to the finer things, such as aesthetics and fashion sense, they love to feature an overly Spanish "national" dress, which only looks good on a mestiza like Imelda Marcos, but looks ridiculously voluminous when donned by the Indio. Some observers regard this as the *Philip*pino's continuing attempt to achieve that coveted colonial master's superior looks, which, to the former Indio slave, inalterably conveys a superior status.

This predominant facet of *Philip*pino psychology is a telling symptom of a 'soul collective capture': a people whose collective imagination has been captured. A country which, if it ever comes close to becoming cognizant of how it has long been suffering from identity confusion, will hopefully move towards self-rediscovery. The rediscovery of the underlying *indigenous pulse* that beats in the native hearts of all her various colorful ethnic groups, a pulse that is naturally shared by the countries surrounding her.

In fact, the process that a whole country (with diverse ethnic groups and considerable experience of foreign subjugation) has to undergo to regain a lost identity and reintegrate a divided and conquered soul is no different from the process that each individual inhabitant of that country (who is inherently multifaceted and has experienced degrees of humiliation and disempowerment) has to undergo in his or her search for meaning, quest for freedom and personal wholeness.

31

TO FIND ONE'S SELF

Years of dreaming about traveling, and in my restlessness to find whatever I thought I was looking for, I decided to embark on a vision quest. With my savings from my previous corporate job, I set out backpacking to neighboring countries. One can only imagine the exhilaration I felt. After years confined to toiling inside a vertical box building, in a rectangular box room, in a squarish box cubicle, communing daily with a box machine, I found myself free and out on the open wide road, soaking up the sun, delighting in foreign scenery, relishing exotic tastes, and meeting many more social misfits like me. Traveling felt so right, so fun, and educational, that I wanted it to last forever. I wished I did not have to go back to work, ever again. Then my wish was granted.

Four months into my solo journey, just as I was about to run out of travel funds and was dreading the prospect of having to rejoin the labor camp sooner or later, a newfound friend who described himself as a 'longtime traveler' invited me to continue traveling with him. Unlike me, who had to work for my money, he is one of the few exceptions, as he does not have to toil for a living. He has enough inheritance to live the life he desires.

After nearly two years of traveling, however, living a life of adventure on the road unpredictably lost its novelty. Although my previous structured working life appeared to be the very opposite of my now freewheeling traveling life, I started to notice patterns of my old reality show-up when familiar feelings of restlessness and weariness began to arise. Forcing myself to wake up in the middle of the night or very early in the morning to catch rides for the next travel destination suddenly resembled my agonizing effort to get out of bed each morning to go to work. Riding on crowded trains and chasing running buses began to resemble the daily scuffle I used to endure during rush hours when I commuted to work. The long hours spent waiting in bus and ferry terminals and airport lounges felt like the times I spent waiting for boring business meetings to finish. Eating mostly instant and street food while on the road was not very different from a stressed-out yuppie's unhealthy eating habits. And, as I used to be burdened by what I personally felt was a meaningless task in my previous job, I felt that the backpack I carried around became heavier as each day passed. My life on the road had also become tedious and tiring. I again started to ask questions: Where am I going? Where would I like to go? *What is the purpose of my indefinite journey?*

I came to realize that I was, in fact, living a parallel existence – a seemingly different way of living life, but which was actually only a different version of the life I thought I had left behind. This was my metaphysical excuse, or explanation, for why I had lost my enthusiasm to go on traveling. My longtime traveling friend, who had been sponsoring my travel since I teamed up with him, had a different explanation: he said that I got tired of traveling simply because the lucky, whiny brat in me became *lazy* about repeatedly packing and unpacking my luggage.

Unlike me, my friend showed no signs of wanting to stop wandering. Although he had been on the 'travel path' for many years already, he was restless and wanted to go everywhere he possibly could. The Moon is the limit, he told me.

"To what end do you travel? What do you gain if you reach the ends of the earth?" I asked him.

"I travel to find my *self*," he answered.

Through my travel experience, I know that life is truly analogous to traveling. Just like my impression of life, which I have come to know as drudgery, I felt that flitting from one physical location to another had become like an aimless chore. I began to wonder what the point of my long and continuous journey everywhere, yet nowhere in particular, was. To *find one's own self*? Based on my own experience and observations of other travelers, leaving home to find one's self turned out to be a very tricky process. Traveling can also be exhausting and distracting. Hence, traveling the world in an attempt to find one's self, is unlikely to yield the desired results if the busy, distracted, and weary traveler is unable to spare enough energy and gather enough focus to also *travel inwards*. Although the benefits of traveling cannot be emphasized enough, I realized that it is not a necessity to leave home to go 'looking for one's self' in other places, or in other people. One need not reach India, or the Moon, to find one's self.

I have to admit, though, the paradox that perhaps if I had not left home and wandered around, I would not have discovered the truth that one's self is not found someplace else, but is found wherever one is, at the moment. It was then that I understood what the sages meant when they said, "Right where you are – be still – and find your *self*".

"Traveling is my life," my travel companion told me. Again, I guess, just like in our routinized lives, once in a while, we have to take a break from 'pulling' and 'pushing' in our daily toil; and in our freewheeling travels, we need to take a break from 'coming' and 'going' in order to reflect on our restlessness, and to take some moments to ask ourselves if what we are busily preoccupied with is moving us closer to our dreams, or to whatever it is we want to create. The thing is, again, just like in life, I noticed that many longtime travelers, such as my friend, did not actually have a dream or a goal. Many, including me, were not clear about what we were wanting. So we just went on drifting from one place to another, like a ship without a rudder, at the mercy of the wind. More than the motivation to leave home to find one's self, I realized that some of us, long-time travelers, had felt compelled to leave home to avoid something or to run away from some unpleasant situations at home.

I was quite surprised myself when I found out that I wanted to go back to work! When I expressed this to my friend, he said that, unlike me, financial matters were not his 'life's challenge', so he did not see any need to work and become a slave to the system. For me, however, 'work' took on an entirely new and different meaning. This time, I wanted to work, not for survival reasons, but because there arose a yearning within me to *create*, or to give birth to something that would bring me greater personal fulfillment.

I, nonetheless, had no idea what it was I wanted to create. I had no clue what would bring me personal fulfillment. I only knew that going back to the usual toil was not what I desired. Besides, in a fast-paced and fiercely competitive world, I knew that I was already considered a left-behind in the rat race.

Once again, I was back to a point where I had no idea what to do, or where to go. Then one night, while on a bus ride to somewhere, I had the following dream:

I was driving a huge white bus. I was the only one inside the bus, and although my hands were on the steering wheel, I did not have any control over it. I felt helpless and trapped inside the bus as it was tossed back and forth and in circles. With one last push forward, I saw that I was going to fall into a deep ravine. I stiffened, bracing myself for the worst. But in an instant, instead of falling into the ravine, I saw myself standing outside the bus. Mother was standing right in front of me. She 'chewed' the head of Apu which appeared to be like a big fish's head. Then she handed me the compact part of the fish-like head. I took it, dismantled it, and extracted an even smaller object. It was a bone-like substance encasing what appeared to be a silvery metal. Then Mother said, "That is the core of Ina's skull. If you want, take it and add it to what you have". Then I saw that, on my other hand, I was clutching pieces of small, colorful crystalline stones. I dropped the 'core', and the stones into my knitted childhood sling pouch, which I noticed was slung over my shoulder.

I woke up to find myself inside a passenger bus negotiating a very rough dirt road. I looked out the window; it was very dark. There were no lights in the distance, which meant we were passing by an uninhabited territory. All I could see were the dark outlines of trees and foliage, and I could hear the grumbling of gravel being crushed by the tires of the bus. That night, as I sat quietly looking out the window, I experienced a very deep, peaceful feeling which I had not felt in a very long time.

Although I had earlier wished to travel for life, the unanticipated happened. I had lost interest in a life of privileged wandering. I did not judge such a "hedonistic" lifestyle to be, in any way, morally inferior to any other preferred lifestyle. And I felt no guilt in taking it a little too easy while the rest of the world toiled away to earn their daily bread. But I soon found out that a privileged non-working lifestyle could equally feel as empty as a hard worker's lifestyle is.

My travel friend and I came to a point where we both agreed that we do not share the same ideas on how to travel in life. So, like a river, I broke off from another shared life-flow to follow a different trail. I let my friend continue to find himself in his travels, as I hoped to find myself in my true labor of love.

32

ENLIGHTENMENT

I had a very disturbing, yet very enlightening vision. The totality of the vision is ineffable, to say the least. It came as a plethora of sensations, images, impressions, and thoughts that simultaneously played out in my bewildered perception.

I just woke up from an afternoon nap. I did not know how long exactly the nap was as I did not check the time before and after I napped. It could have lasted from 30 minutes to over an hour. When I awoke, I saw through the window that it was already late in the afternoon. The mountain tops were aglow with the sun's amber rays. Summoned by the compelling spectacle outside, I got up and walked towards the fully opened window. I sat on the window sill, where a gentle, warm, and refreshing breeze met me. The colors of nature appeared to vibrate. The flowers on a nearby hill seemed to glow under the muted shine of the sun. The very calm shore shimmered silver-gray. A very deep sense of peace permeated my entire being – a sensation which seemed to extend towards my surroundings. Or it could also be that it was the beautiful surrounding nature that reverberated deep serenity and it enveloped me. It was impossible to pinpoint the source of this exceptionally peaceful sensation.

I dreamily watched as the big orange sun slowly descended over the horizon. At a certain moment, however, I felt that within the depth of the serenity I was experiencing, also came profound sorrow. I surmised that the reason for my sorrow was because the sun was slowly leaving, and soon it would be the passing of yet another day. I was, at that time, on a paradise island, but had become weary of drifting from one exotic beach to another like a piece of debris in the ocean. Yet the lack of any idea about what I was going to do for my personal fulfillment, and more importantly, the bugging question of what I was here on Earth for, had been making me melancholic each time I saw the fading colors of the sunset.

The idea that I was placed on Earth in order to toil, as a punishment for what I believed was a divinely sanctioned 'human error', which I or my ancestors had committed in the distant past sounded absurd and ridiculous whenever I thought of it. I saw no great intelligence behind the intent of a God to put people on Earth to struggle to work hard, to fight and compete with one another for resources just so they could "earn their right to exist". On top of that, they are expected to both worship and fear a *great unknown*, whom they call God, lest they will be, again, punished or condemned to eternally burn in a lake of fire.

When I emailed my friend Mercy, telling her my change of heart regarding traveling and my intention to go back home and do something more personally fulfilling, she wrote back, telling me that perhaps what I needed was to get married. She theorized that my urge to create or produce something more personally fulfilling was simply my biological need to produce progeny. In my reply to her, I pointed out the fact that our country has an oversupply of people compared to the demand for them, and this situation is apparently making us susceptible to cheap labor exploitation. I did not want to add another laborer to the cheap labor colony. Furthermore, if a progeny were to ask why he or she was born, I wanted to be prepared to give a more satisfying answer rather than simply repeat what my own mother had told me – that she didn't know why, or that we were born because God wanted some creatures to worship and sing praises to Him.

As I sat, in a contemplative mood, by the window sill, the combined moods of stillness, sorrow, and emptiness became increasingly oppressive. The vehemence enfolded within this mélange of poignant sensations agonized every fiber of my being, as if it were tearing me apart. I struggled to trace the origin of this harrowing sensation. What I immediately perceived was the dreadful, disturbing feeling of being caught in a trap!

Trapped in a seemingly endless cycle of life and death with no way out, a multitude of indistinct forms of beings, myself included, are in a deep, dark pit. Some of those in the pit appeared to be looking up, either wondering about what was up there in the open, or desiring to emerge from the dark hole, which had the feeling of being a trap. But many seemed to be either unconcerned or unaware that they were in a deep, dark pit. Within that pit-trap-like realm, however, there was a sense that anyone was capable and allowed to do whatever they wanted, and that there were no limits to what they could do or become, except that they could not get out of the trap – because there appeared to be no way out of the trap. A line from a popular rock song kept playing in the back of my mind: "You can check out anytime you like, but you can never leave." There was a horrible feeling that nothing was new inside the pit trap. Everyone is merely repeating different facets of, perhaps, a million different patterns.

An enormous and continuous stream of ideas, sensations, diaphanous thoughts, and supple images bombarded my consciousness with 'knowledge' or 'information'. It was overwhelming and bewildering. I felt dizzy and nauseous. I went to lie down on the bed, but as I lay down, I felt suffocated. I was having difficulty breathing. It was not because there was not enough room in that pit-trap-like realm; it was just that I felt like I was drowning all the time, and in order to not drown, I had to constantly struggle to keep my head afloat. It soon appeared that the drowning sensation was because I seemed to forget to breathe, and by the time the feeling of discomfort or suffocation reached my consciousness, I tended to remember to quickly gasp for air.

I was in the middle of one of these gasping moments when it

dawned on me that the repetitiousness happening inside the pit trap was meaningless and empty. And I realized that the sensation of being ensnared in a *repetitive cycle*, in a dark, pit-like-trap, with no way out, was the underlying source of the angst and emptiness that seemed to gnaw at every fiber of my being.

After initially putting up some resistance, I resigned myself to a vision which appeared to unfold beyond my control. In the midst of the volume of impressions playing out in my perception, I initially found it difficult to focus on a specific train of thought. But at times, it seemed that certain thoughts, images, or sensations made themselves more prominent, and my attention seemed to follow or dwell on such more dominant thoughts, impressions, or feelings. When this happened, the particular impression, sensation, or thought I focused upon became even more emphasized, or vivified, to the extent that it appeared to 'solidify' into reality. As these more focused moments happened, bizarre, mind-bending perceptions were gleaned.

Not necessarily perceived or received in a sequential order, for there appeared to be no particular order at all, the more striking sensations include the following:

I suddenly felt like a very old but wise woman. I looked at my hands and my feet and, to my horror, I saw that my skin had turned coarse and wrinkled. Even as I moved my body, the way I thought, how I behaved, were all unmistakably those of an old hag. Although the old woman appeared to be wise, I was very frightened, not because I am an unbeliever in the unexplainable – including, but not limited to the possibility of some sort of sorcery that somebody on that remote island might have maliciously inflicted on me – but because I was afraid of how people would react if they saw me suddenly and inexplicably old.

At that moment, I thought I was going to die. Even as I was mentally preparing myself for my impending death, I was consciously concerned about other people's opinions regarding my bizarre transformation and then sudden death. I was in a remote foreign place with only my travel friend who knew me. I thought: if I died here in this condition right now, what would people think? How would my friend explain to my family back home that I suddenly died looking like an old hag?

Alarmed by my mysterious transformation, I gathered my will to counter the sensation of being an old woman. I firmly thought to myself that I knew I was a young woman and not the very old woman I had suddenly become. As soon as I thought of myself as being a young woman, I turned into a youthful, bubbly adolescent. In my perception at that moment, I felt and looked like a fifteen-year-old. Then I saw that, as a young woman, I was acting like an actor on a stage. Although I was previously conscious of the presence of lights in the opposite distant village, at that moment, in my perception, when I became an actor, the lights in the opposite village appeared to be spotlights or a crowd of audience cheering for me. I had the impression that I was a well-known character. I was popular and liked, as evidenced by the applauding audience. The more they applauded, the more I bloomed like a proud blossom. I kept my head up. I constantly beamed a smile at myself and at my audience. My movements and bearing were graceful and elegant. I felt good, confident, and full of energy.

It did not take very long when I sensed that my neck kept on sagging, causing my head to droop. As this happened, I involuntarily turned into that old hag again! To counteract this, I discovered that when I *consciously* and deliberately held my chin up and kept my head up, I could transform back into that vivacious adolescent. I was totally spooked about being a strange old woman, so I kept on holding my head up while I paced the room in sheer bewilderment. After a while, I got tired of keeping my head raised as it also felt heavier. I sensed my vivacity declining, and I became considerably weak. Again, alarmed by this weakening sensation, I told myself firmly and consciously that I was strong. At once, I was again reinvigorated. I also found out that when I simply held the thought, 'keep the energy up', the energy surged in an instant. I was amazed at how easily the energy shifted, from high to low or to wherever I directed it with my thoughts.

One of the images that occurred in my mind was the character of Angelina Jolie in her Tomb Raider movie. Dwelling on that particular image, I instantaneously and distinctly sensed the muscles in my shoulders and arms bulging. Suddenly, I felt big, tall, sexy, a very powerful woman. I was dumbfounded, intimidated by my own (or by the character's) apparent power. But that sensation did not last long as my thoughts drifted on to Julia Roberts, at which point, I felt myself quietly crying. Despite myself, I could feel tears streaming down my cheeks, as if I were in an emotionally charged situation. At this point, my travel friend came in, sat on a chair, and started strumming his mandolin. Embarrassed to be seen in such an awkward situation, I avoided facing him. My attempt to contain or to stop crying, however, was made impossible by the sensation of tears that continued to roll down my cheeks.

A conscious part of me was very much aware that I was not being myself – that I was morphing into different personalities that came to mind. My conscious awareness of my remaining sanity scared me even more because of the thought that I might have gone permanently mad. Eventually, I turned to my friend and asked him how he thought I looked. He appeared to be a bit confused as he glanced up at me. I was standing and he was sitting on a chair. For a second or two, he looked at me in the face, then quickly scanned my entire body by moving only his eyes, up, down, and up again. He shrugged and plainly said, "Why? You look like you". I was half relieved and half puzzled by his answer. Then I said to him, "Let's say you are Johnny Depp". "Ok, I am Johnny Depp," he laughed, playing along. Instantaneously, within my perception, he started behaving as if he were Johnny Depp in the Pirates of the Caribbean movie! My friend had dreadlocks like the pirate Jack Sparrow, but he didn't have a mustache like the pirate. However, when he became Jack Sparrow, he acquired a mustache, and a red bandanna was wrapped around his head! I was so amazed that I could not stop laughing, until a slightly annoyed and puzzled Jack Sparrow stood up and left. Immediately, a light bulb lit up and my late Grandma's words rang clearly in my ears: "I will tell you the truth; a real story is the one you think or believe to be a real story." Even though it made no rational sense at that time, I just knew those words were true!

The thought of a particular girl friend, whom I used to judge as stubborn and emotional, crossed my mind. She had been bothering me with her endless lamentations about her breakup with her boyfriend. I had been avoiding her because I knew she wouldn't listen to anything I had to say. But in that split second when I thought of her, I *became her*. And I could clearly feel how she was feeling! It also appeared that I was thinking her thoughts. As the embodiment of her, I felt a lot of conflicting and yearning emotions inside me. And since I could vividly feel what she was going through, I found myself unable to criticize or judge her in the same way I used to. Despite this sensation, I was still aware of myself as distinct from her. There were two personalities inside me: my girl friend's and myself. As her personality, I was fully feeling her churning emotions and pain. As my own personality, I was witnessing myself as her!

My thoughts turned to another friend I hadn't seen in a long time and who I had been keeping a secret from. I had always assumed that if he found out about my secret, he would be furious with me. As I thought of him, I saw an image of his face, and I had a sudden realization that he, in fact, already knew my secret down to the smallest detail. Despite the fact that I could see his face in front of me, I had the distinct impression that he was not truly separate from my being. His face smiled, and through thought communication, he confirmed that he knew my secret and that everything was fine because it was just the way it was that I kept a secret from him. I was very relieved to learn that he was not angry with me or my secret.

At that point, it occurred to me that no one could truly conceal anything from anyone else. Secrets, or hidden information, are unreal or illusory because it appears that people are not truly separate, or that people are linked at some fundamental levels, allowing anyone to know what one knows.

Even though my trepidation did not totally disappear, I felt like a magician. I had the urge to experiment. When I deliberately thought of 'miracles', I immediately felt very powerful – as if I could walk on water, speak and understand foreign languages, or pick-up any musical instrument and play it like a virtuoso. I picked up my friend's mandolin and strummed it. The sound it produced did not please my ears. I sensed that the instrument and I were not in sync.

Strangely enough, I held a strong conviction that I could sweep my hands on the sick, intend healing, and an illness would be gone in no time. The thoughts of poverty, sickness, and germs occurred in my mind. A cluster of 'germs' with a form presented itself in my mind's eye. I felt that I could just blow air on the cluster and it would magically disperse and disappear into nothing. So I blew on the 'cluster of germs', and it vanished as I thought it would. But, there was a nagging feeling in the back of my mind that the germ cluster wasn't really there to begin with. This thought caused me to question whether the cluster of germs that appeared in my mind's eye was real, or not.

The moment I entertained the idea that sickness and germs might not really exist, it felt as if they truly had no real or solid existence in my perception at that time. It appeared that sickness and germs were only ideas that took on certain shapes and even colors as we imagined them, or as we converged our thoughts on them. Sickness and germs seemed to be concepts or 'entities' that could be quarantined in a separate file or designated to exist in another space and time. This was, admittedly, a very weird impression, but at that moment, the impression felt correct, and valid.

The thought of 'healing' occurred in my mind. I perceived an image or an idea of a sick person. The pair of legs was especially emphasized. The legs were supposed to be afflicted with a certain disease or injury. It felt very easy to heal the illness because the body appeared transparent like glass yet soft, fibrous, and elastic, unlike glass. And what was considered to be the disease affecting the legs could simply be 'plucked', or swept away with a single (or two or more, if preferred) intentional sweep of a healer's hand. But then again, somewhere in the recesses of my awareness remained the thought that the disease was *substantially nonexistent* in the first place, and nothing was really wrong with that transparent fibrous form despite it being believed and even diagnosed to be with a certain disease. This was how contradictory this impression appeared to be, but beyond the perception of my reasoning mind at that time, there was really no contradiction.

And since it appeared to me on that occasion that, like sickness and germs, poverty is another condition that forms in the mind, I thought of myself as very wealthy. In an instant, I practically felt and behaved as if I were one of the richest characters in the world. I was energized and exhilarated by the sensation. Then I had a subtle understanding that it is, in fact, neither difficult nor impossible to be very rich, or to be whatever I want to be. Wealth and poverty, like sickness and germs, appeared to be also only ideas we hold in our minds. I then realized that by constantly holding a belief or an image of oneself – whether that of being rich or poor – the belief, idea, or image might just *solidify* into tangible reality.

With the thought of *money* occurring in my mind, I was spontaneously transported back in time to my childhood: I was standing by the doorway. It was a cold and overcast Christmas day. A family guest who had just left gave me an old, large one-peso coin. Mother was asking me to give her the coin, so she could keep it for me. I refused. I wanted to buy some candy with it. The one-peso coin could buy me a handful of candies, which I would be proud to show off and share with my brothers and playmates. As if it were the candy I was planning to buy, I put the coin in my mouth and toyed with it with my tongue. Mother noticed what I was doing. "That's filthy!" she exclaimed. Before I could understand Mother's strong reaction, and before I could spit the coin out, she grabbed my chin and forcibly extracted the coin with her fingers. She flung the coin as if it were a little evil monster. I touched my chin; it hurt. She poked my cheek with her fingers, and my head jerked to the opposite side. "How many times have I told you not to put money in your mouth? It has passed through many people's hands, and it is very dirty!" Mother scolded me. She left for the fields in a rush.

She was very upset with me. I was left alone in the house. It was very quiet. I could hear my soft sobbing. In between sobs, I glanced at the old one-peso coin that had landed and was partially hidden behind a biscuit tin can where we store rice grains. I heard it speak: "I am not dirty. I was invented by humans, and was tasked and expected to do my job. I am the thing you use to buy your clothing, your shoes, your candy, and other things you need. I am not dirty." The coin sounded very offended.

As Apu would put it, it was the 'spirit' of money that spoke. Indeed, I could not understand why Mother always said that money was dirty when I observed that she and Father seemed to put so much value in it. Mother wrapped money bills and old coins in a colorful handkerchief that she kept hidden in a corner of her closet. Father never gave out money easily. Whenever my elder siblings asked for money from Father, I often heard him tell them that they should not think that money was easy to find and easy to give away. Money, then, appeared to me to be an object hard to obtain, yet very important and very desirable, that I was so confused as to why such a valuable thing was also considered very dirty.

The ongoing vision seemed to convey the idea that money, like everything else, is only an *idea*. The idea of money was indeed conceived by humans to serve a particular purpose. I then understood that any object, such as money, only becomes valuable and desirable when a collective of people agree to assign a value to it; otherwise, money is just a piece of paper or metal.

As I was gaining confidence and lucidity in the midst of the transpiring dreamlike vision or hallucination, I consciously wished to find an answer to the mystery of God. I thought of 'God', the Creator of all things. The very simple response, in the form of an idea or a thought that occurred, suggested that there is no God, but that there is only us, and that we are in a pit trap! Inexplicably, within my state of perception at that moment, this blasphemous idea also made perfect sense!

I thought of the Buddha. I remembered that somebody had once told me that when the Buddha attained enlightenment, he ascended to the highest heavens because he was free of any earthly desire and attachment that might keep him from returning to earth. Yet another person contended that the Buddha has not yet ascended to the highest heavens because he cannot do so without everyone else, and that he is waiting for the rest of us to catch up so that we can all ascend together to the highest heavens. At that moment, when I thought of the Buddha, the immediate impression I received was that the Buddha had, in fact, left, yet had not, in fact, left. He is around, nearby, yet also somewhere else, distant. He is out of the pit trap, yet still in the pit trap! And then, as if to make the vague even more nebulous, I got the impression that the above ambiguous perception regarding the Buddha's whereabouts was irrelevant.

Of all the concepts I entertained while within that altered state of consciousness, the impression regarding the Buddha's whereabouts was the hardest for me to grasp. In retrospect, my analytical mind came up with three possible interpretations of the ambiguity. First, that the Buddha may have been indeed freed and thus unconstrained to come and go, in and out of the pit trap.

Becoming Mad and Asking Why the River is Flowing

Second, 'truth' is not fixed, but capricious and compliant according to the perspective and belief of the perceiver of truth. Third, my difficulty in understanding this particular impression of the Buddha was simply perhaps because the attributes of a Buddha are beyond my mind's grasp, even in that state of heightened perception.

At times, I felt drowsy, my eyelids becoming heavy. My head was becoming heavy. I resisted the urge to lie down and sleep because when I did, the sensation of drowning and suffocation came upon me even more intensely. Ironically, no matter how omnipotent and perked up I felt as a result of the magic I could seem to perform, and despite the infinite information or knowledge I could seem to absorb, lurking somewhere in the background was the abysmal sorrow and emptiness, ready to dominate my awareness any time I gave in to these sensations. A persistent 'so what' question bothered me: So what if I am supremely beautiful? So what if I am very wealthy and popular? So what if I can amass a massive amount of information or knowledge? As soon as I directed my thoughts towards being younger, more beautiful, and richer, as soon as I felt my omniscience, *I became what I thought*, only to be quickly reminded that I was trapped in a dark hole with no way out.

I felt stuck with the morbid impression that, while we have the freedom and free will to be whoever we want to be, we are only repeating – over and over – what felt like an endless, tiresome, and meaningless cycle, regardless of how pleasant or unpleasant the experiences we are having. I was brooding over this particular impression when I distinctly felt how my eyelids blinked, in a very slow motion. Simultaneous with the blink, the image of the unmoving, deep, dark, and stale water of the River Kok flashed, momentarily, in my mind. I shuddered as I realized something nightmarish: being trapped and drowning in deep, dark, stale, and static water is not only dangerous, but it can be the most depressing state one can ever find themselves in.

Then I saw an old woman, and next to her was an old man. They were sitting quietly in two separate chairs at the end of a narrow wooden pier. The atmosphere was cold, grayish with fog, and the elderly couple were dressed in thick blue-gray jackets. Then I became aware that this old woman was, in fact, me. The man and I were gazing silently at the distant horizon, across a very calm sea or lake. The opposite side of the sea or the lake was made invisible by a thick mist. There were no waves or movement on the surface of the water. It was a chilly, overcast day, and an eerie stillness abounded. I understood that we were sitting there simply because there was nothing else for us to do, nowhere else for us to go. We have reached the terminal phase of our lives and are waiting for the inevitable – death. But paradoxically, even as this fatalistic thought was passing vividly through my head, I was simultaneously having the opposite thought – the thought that we could *not* really die. There was a foreboding feeling that we would be recycled back to life – to repeat the same circular patterns of existence all over again. Struck by this sensation, I suddenly felt the power of the invisible trap tightening its grip on me. Another mighty wave of haunting sadness and great emptiness washed over me; harsh and brutally honest, the wave slapped me with the 'information' that what we call 'death' is not and will not be the end. Death is not the way out of the invisible trap we have fallen into.

Then it crossed my mind: if death is not the gateway to liberation, if it is not the event that will bring an end to human suffering, what are heaven and hell, the places where we are believed to go after we die? As soon as the above question hit me, I had the perception that I was no longer in my body. I simply lost the sense of having a material body or a physical anchor. I had the sensation of floating, like air; light and expansive, unrestricted. I appeared to have the natural and spontaneous ability to 'fly,' 'float,' or simply exist wherever I desired. I could *will* myself to be anywhere and be there in an instant. And then, passing like a momentary spark in my awareness, it occurred to me *who* I am. It appeared that what I thought of as 'me' was merely a transitory thought; a fleeting dream – an ephemeral idea belonging to a bigger thought or idea within consciousness. This bigger thought or idea within consciousness also belongs to an even bigger thought or idea within an even bigger consciousness – and the pattern goes on like that, through infinity.

Yet, even as a mere incorporeal thought or idea within consciousness, I still felt drowning, suffocated. Even without my body, I did not feel released from the weight or from the pull of the pit trap. And then I heard, lucidly, the words, *'on earth as it is in heaven,'* being recited in a chorus – in a hypnotic, prayerful manner. Accompanying those words, images of the countless novenas for the dead that I often attended with Mother when I was a small child flashed graphically through my mind. At that very same instant, those enigmatic words, without doubt, purported the meaning: *what you lose on earth, you lose in heaven*. Again, as I blinked, I felt another instance of enlightenment, as I clearly felt I had finally grasped the meaning of that cryptic passage which had so confounded Mother and me.

I heard a most soothing music. Very lithe and svelte beings, who appeared to be floating and looked like humans, were playing unidentifiable musical instruments through their mouths. They were dressed in pastel-colored body-fitting garments with intricate designs. I had the impression that all shades of color adorned their dresses, although soft pink, light blue, and violet or lavender were more noticeable. There was a sense that they belonged to a very ancient time, yet they also exuded the ambiance of eternity as they did not appear to have disappeared, and it did not seem likely that they would cease to exist at any future time. As a separate entity, I could objectively observe them as if I were watching a play taking place around me. Yet I also seemed to be a part of the play as I virtually felt like one of them. The celestial music was movingly familiar, yet I could not name, compare, or associate it with anything I had ever heard before. The music evoked the feeling of an infinitely deep, boundless, nostalgic peace. In retrospect, I consider this to be the most heavenly episode in the entire vision.

Intrigued by the mysterious impressions about *past, present, and future*, I thought about 'time'. But as soon as I thought about time, time stood still! It was as if the globe, the planets, and the stars had all come to a halt. Everything rolled to a standstill . . . in perfect balance . . . in utter silence . . . space, time, and everything else that was thought to exist – appeared to disappear.

In one eternal, timeless moment, **There Is – No Thing.**

♥ ♥ ♥

What came next was a blur. The last thing I remembered was sitting on the window sill, staring blankly out the window at the still dark night, and yet, within my mental vision, I was perceiving a plethora of images and sensations: thought forms that were fleeting yet grandiose, capricious yet highly coordinated.

33

THE WICKED AUNT

"Wake-up, wake-up, let's go!" I felt somebody shaking me in the dark. I made out the figure of my travel companion looking down at me. He was shaking my shoulder. I was about to protest when he reproached me for having slept without packing my things the previous night. I glanced at the clock on the wall, which read 4:05 in the morning. I was reminded that we were going to move at 5:30 in the morning that day. I heard my friend say that he tried to wake me the night before, but I was sleeping as if I were dead.

I felt tired and was having difficulty focusing. I forced myself out of bed and made my way to the washroom. I felt lightheaded with a dull ache in my head. As I was quickly gathering my things to pack, I noticed the white sleeveless top that a certain local woman had specially requested that I give her as a gift the day before. Together with the white top, I put another thin, cream-colored blouse in a plastic bag. Though the woman only asked to have the white top, I thought that the other blouse I was giving away to her would actually suit her better.

After a quick breakfast of fresh fruits, dried nuts, and oatmeal, I went to the reception desk and asked Sarah, the young woman in charge of the guest house, if a certain elderly lady had come to see me the night before. Sarah said she closed at around midnight and before that, nobody came to see me. I then told her that a woman from a certain shop would be coming to pick up a package from me, and asked if she could kindly pass it on to her. I described the woman from a certain small tourist shop, located not more than two kilometers away from Sarah's guest house. I was sure that the said woman would show up because she sounded determined when she said she would. Sarah said that she knew the shop I was referring to, as well as some of the people who work there, but she was unable to identify the specific elderly woman I described to her. Her uncertainty about the woman perplexed me. I expected that in such a small island town, as is usually the case in small local places, everyone, especially those in the tourism business, would be at least acquainted with one another. She offered to take the package herself to the shop if nobody came to pick it up. I thanked her. Then my friend and I went to the bus terminal for our next travel destination.

The minibus was packed. We had made advance reservations, so we were able to sit in front, next to the driver. We had a twelve-hour bus ride to the city we were heading to, plenty of time for me to piece together the previous day's very strange vision. I glanced at my unsuspecting companion. He was gazing straight ahead at the road. I knew that he would not believe me if I told him what happened the night before.

All in all, the vision was a frightening but enlightening experience. In the back of my mind, the thought lingered that I either had a bout of insanity or that I had been accidentally enlightened. As a result of the vision, random ideas, phrases, idioms, and aphorisms that had previously been unclear to me have become clear and meaningful. The profundity of certain abstractions, which I had previously only superficially grasped, became self-evident. Age-old conundrums resolved themselves in the most natural, yet subtle manner. All thoughts, sensations, impressions, images, etc., were like a million pieces of a colossal jigsaw puzzle naturally coming together to form a very coherent story. Paradoxically, however, in spite of my purported elucidation, all of my efforts to understand how the vision came to be were futile.

I was drifting in and out of sleep when I suddenly remembered a very unusual dream I had the night before. True to her word, the elderly woman who so much wanted the white sleeveless top as a gift from me, in fact, came to Sarah's guest house that very same night she said she would come. She came with a small woven rattan basket with a lid. The basket was small enough that only one hand could fit through the opening. She was in her usual jovial mood, telling me something I could no longer recall. The dream seemed to have ended when she handed me the small basket, telling me not to open it until 'it is time', or until something in particular happened. The texture of this dream was distinct from other dreams I considered to have consequential meaning. This dream was not vivid, but rather ethereal.

Upon suddenly remembering that I had this odd dream, I opened my eyes. Though the connection appeared to be incredible, I wondered if the woman's *gift* of a basket had anything to do with the bizarre vision that took place in the early evening of that day.

I recollected the events prior to the occurrence of the vision. On that particular day, my travel friend and I did not do any sightseeing as it was our last day on the island and we just wanted to take it easy before taking the long twelve-hour bus ride to our next stop. My friend had eaten his lunch at around noon, but as I did not feel hungry, I did not join him for lunch. I felt hungry around two o'clock in the afternoon, so I went around looking for a place to eat. I walked along the beach until I arrived at the location of this particular elderly woman's tourist shop and food stall. She was previously introduced to us by another traveler who had earlier joined one of her package tours. She was doing business by organizing visits and activities to the different sightseeing destinations on the island. After our introduction to her, we joined one of her boat tours. During our two-week stay in that island town, we also approached her when we needed information or other types of assistance. However, despite the several interactions we had with her, we never had the chance to know her name, as we never bothered to ask. We simply went on addressing her by the general polite term, 'auntie'.

Three or four small, dented aluminum pots were lined up on the counter top of her food stall, which was made of split bamboo and sticks. I opened the pots; there was scarcely any food left. She emerged from the back room with her characteristic beam. She said I was twenty-five minutes too late. There were bigger restaurants around the area, but it would take some time for them to prepare food orders. I told her that I was famished and asked if she could direct me to another place where they sold ready-to-eat food, so I did not have to wait for my order to be prepared. She responded by saying that she had just cooked a special and exotic dish. In her most convincing but playful manner of talking, she said that the food was simple but very nutritious, and that she cooked it just for herself. Then she said she might share the leftovers with me if I was 'in the mood' for it. I answered OK. She was standing at the door leading to the back room, one arm leaning against the wall to support her weight and the other hand propped up around her waist. She stood there for several moments, studying me with a slight smile and a mischievous gleam in her eyes. Talking with my travel friend about her, I always referred to her as 'the wicked aunt' because of her habit of spontaneously cracking up wicked jokes, and her total lack of inhibition to laugh wickedly at her own wicked jokes. My friend preferred to call her 'the crazy aunt' for her crazy antics. We found her to be a very funny woman who was also quite eccentric.

She disappeared into the back room, then came back with a small clay pot. She carefully poured the contents of the pot into a coconut shell bowl. Motioning with her chin, she signaled me to go and take my seat on one of the bamboo benches outside, under the shade of palm trees. A few minutes later, she came, carrying a tray. On the tray were a very small portion of cooked rice, a rather small slice of fish, and a generous amount of a soupy viand of unfamiliar mixed vegetables. She placed the food on the table in front of me, and I immediately went for it. I thought she would leave me alone to eat, but she just stood there, watching me. I looked at her. She appeared to be either surprised or concerned about the way I was devouring the food. "Slowly," she said in a serious tone. Since her 'special' and 'exotic' viand, which I assumed was the mixed vegetables, tasted and looked anything but special and exotic, I asked her, half in jest, how the viand was supposed to be special and exotic as she claimed it to be. She replied that it was special because it was not eaten as frequently as regular food. "It is a seasonal food that requires special preparation and is normally consumed only on special occasions," she said gaily. She then sat down next to me. I could feel her gaze on me as she watched me eat. She remained quiet until I finished my meal. I felt uncomfortable with the way she was prying on me, but I dismissed her behavior as an unconscious habit of some locals who tend to forwardly and inquisitively stare at strangers. When I was done eating, she slid even closer. She pinched and pulled the white sleeveless top I was wearing, saying it was lovely and she liked it. She asked me if I could give it to her as a *gift*. I was about to laugh at her strange request, but I held back for fear of embarrassing her. I initially thought that she was, as usual, joking. But I also sensed an air of seriousness about her, which was rather unusual. It made me wonder if she really wanted the shirt.

The sleeveless white top I was wearing was certainly not for an elderly village woman like her. I think she was maybe in her sixties. She had a sweet, round, smiley face, a bit plump in body size, and of short stature. The sleeveless white top had a plunging neckline. The backside was even more low-cut, connected and decorated by a crisscross of thin straps. It was a stylish, sultry top that young ladies in the city would wear, so I did not think it would be appropriate for her. I wondered if she was considering giving it as a gift to someone else, perhaps a young daughter or a niece. And it was not even brand-new clothing. She commented, as if she could read my unspoken thoughts, that the shirt was stretchable and would fit her. I found her opinion preposterous. It was certainly stretchable and could fit her, but was she going to wear it while running her small business in that charming but very rustic local place? Was she going to wear that shirt while accompanying her guests on island-hopping boat rides and jungle treks? Was she going to wear it to full moon beach parties? I always saw her in a body-fitting long-sleeved blouse and a long, wrap-around sarong skirt. She looked classic in her usual covered attire. Was she going to suddenly change her fashion style for whatever reason that might have occurred to her at that moment? My imagination ran wild trying to figure out when and how a short, chubby, elderly woman would wear a sleeveless top with a plunging neckline and almost backless! Although my impression of her was that she did not behave in accordance with how normal people were expected to behave, it occurred to me, at that time, that she might have been drinking because she looked somewhat inebriated. Her curious request might have been the result of alcohol intoxication. I could smell her because she moved too close next to me, but she did not smell of alcohol; she smelled of smoke. I told her that the white top was also my favorite, and that I would give her another blouse which I was sure would look great on her. She flatly refused, saying she wanted the very same one I was wearing. So I told her that I had just gotten the shirt from someone else and did not want to part with it so soon. She responded that if that was the case, that made it even better for me to pass the shirt on to her also.

"But I am wearing it right now. How will I give it to you?" I said.

"You can bring it here tomorrow," she said.

"We are leaving tomorrow, early," I said.

"Then I'll go to your hotel tonight to pick it up," she said, smiling.

"OK, then." I shrugged, acceding. I couldn't seem to have any more excuses to refuse her.

Some people came to inquire about a tour. She stood up and walked with them towards the small 'tourist shop' adjacent to the food stall. I also stood up to leave. She called after me, reminding me to wait for her that night as she would be coming, and she would be bringing something for me in exchange for the shirt.

I recalled how the white shirt came into my possession, which happened in an equally unusual manner. One evening, after coming back from a full-day excursion, I found the shirt on the table on the veranda of the house we were staying in. It was freshly washed and dried. It was neatly folded, but inside out. Thinking somebody might have mistakenly left or put it there, I hung it on the clothesline outside. The next day, after returning from another day trip, I noticed it was placed on the wooden railings of our veranda. I did not touch it. The next morning, Sarah and a middle-aged man, perhaps her older brother, happened to pass by, and I waved the shirt at them. The man nodded and said that I had dropped the shirt, and he placed it on our veranda. I told them that it was not mine. They seemed to be confused. Sarah pointed out that I was the only one washing clothes by hand and using the clothesline outside, so they assumed it was me who dropped it. I insisted that it was not mine. We agreed to hang it back on the clothesline for the owner, whoever she might be, to notice it. At that time, my friend and I were the longest-staying guests in that guest house compound. Two pairs of young travelers were staying upstairs in a two-story house building, but we rarely saw them because they were always out. I thought that one of the women might own the shirt. In the early morning of their sixth day, however, I saw them check-out, passing by the clotheslines, but without showing even a slight interest in the only clothing that had been hanging there for a couple of days already. After they left, my friend and I were again the only guests remaining. When Sarah came to sweep the front yard, I told her that the guests who had just checked-out did not take the shirt. Sarah told me to better have it, since she thought nobody seemed to own it. I asked why she did not take it for herself instead. She giggled, a little embarrassed, and demurely said that it was too cute for her. That day, I put on the shirt and went to eat a *special exotic meal* at Wicked Aunt's food stall.

34

A SEPARATE JOURNEY

I reached a point where I could no longer keep my hallucinatory vision experience to myself. I took the risk of telling my travel companion about it. He shot me an incredulous look. He asked if my family had a history of depression and mental illness. I told him that, as far as I knew, there had been no cases of mental illness or depression in my family, but I could not be a hundred percent sure because, like me, my mother could be very pensive at times, and my eccentric grandmothers on both sides of my parents could be considered deranged by modern, conventional standards.

I remember when I first met my friend, he was traveling with a group of people who called themselves Rainbow Warriors. When I heard them talk about fairies and magic, animal spirits, and respecting mother nature, I felt an instant affinity with them. They were certainly very different from the people I know. I was fascinated by their lifestyle. They were laid back, creative, and artistic. Nobody was told what to do or how to do it. Following their inspiration, they simply did what they felt like doing and when they felt like doing it.

When my travel friend first talked to me, he told me about a friend of his who had visited my country and traveled to the interior mountain regions of the north, on the island of Luzon, where she had some very interesting encounters with the people she met. When I told him that I come from the same region, he was thrilled. He described our meeting as 'magical,' claiming it was a synchronicity because he was supposed to travel to my country with three of his friends, but for some reason, it did not happen, and he instead found himself in the place where we met. He said he would be honored if I might be the one to take him to my country and be his guide as we explored what he called 'my part of the world'. He expressed an interest in learning more about my people's indigenous beliefs and practices. This was the beginning of our journey together.

My so-called part of the world included Southeast Asia, and he was delighted to discover Southeast Asia with a Southeast Asian. The plan was to start the journey in mainland Southeast Asia from the north, slowly moving downwards to the islands south of the equator, then back up to Borneo. We would take a boat from Borneo to the southern Philippines, then gradually make our way north to Luzon. It would be a slow and leisurely journey.

In the beginning, he was very curious and interested in the new things we were both exploring as we journeyed, both physically and metaphysically, to 'my part of the world'. As we went further and deeper into our journey, however, I increasingly observed that he was not really grasping the deeper meanings or implications of the Asian and indigenous knowledge, culture, and practices that he, at first, said he was keen on learning more about. I got offended when he made light of things I particularly considered should be taken with a little bit more consideration or sensitivity. At a certain point, I became impatient and thought of him as 'slow' for failing to grasp knowledge which I thought was inherent, innate, or common sense, and which did not require extensive verbal explanation or rational debate. In defense, he became increasingly critical and dismissive. He made a mockery of what he said were my strange, unscientific, superstitious, 'oriental beliefs'. But I thought it was mind-boggling how someone could freely talk about fairies, magic, and animal spirits, as if they naturally knew and truly believed in such things, yet readily dismiss a personal and actual account of the same. It was out of guilelessness that I related to him the incident about the crow that talked to me, but never did I expect that telling him that story would cause him to become suspicious of me! He thought I was lying, making up an impossible, preposterous story. Perhaps it was an old childhood wound by those who ridiculed and denied the 'reality' of my experiences, or by those who thought that it came from the 'dark side' – which had been touched by my friend's scorn because I felt betrayed by him – he, who at first presented himself to be interested, open-minded, and even knowledgeable.

The different worldviews, which my friend and I each maintained, gradually created dissonance in our shared journey. It turned out that while we outwardly appeared to be experiencing the same story, inwardly, we were actually experiencing our own separate stories. Although we could be seen walking the same path towards the same destination, we were actually on separate journeys of our own. I believe it was his fear of the unknown or the unfamiliar that made him so hesitant to even temporarily leave 'his familiar part of the world' in order to journey deeper and experience more of 'my part of the world,' which he initially professed to want to discover and know more about.

Long after we parted ways, I realized how inadequate I was as a guide for him in the journey and exploration of 'my part of the world.' It took me a while to grasp Grandma's story about the many different worlds that exist in our midst, and to finally understand and accept that, in a *multi-world reality*, my friend was not necessarily slow. Because in the framework or context of the world in which I was born and raised, some phenomena that are considered natural, normal, or possible are simply regarded as impossible, inconceivable, and even pretentious in my friend's world. Similarly, I believe that telling an unexposed tribal person about the wonders and miracles that computers can perform will elicit the same incredulous response. The unexposed tribal person could think that you are being ridiculous, just plain crazy, or fooling him, as he honestly does not have a reference point in his awareness to imagine a computer machine, let alone what a computer can do! Like my friend, it does not imply that the tribal man or woman is slow or inferior because of his or her inability to comprehend what has never been a part of his or her normal, everyday world-reality.

35

INSIGHTS FROM THE HALLUCINATION

The mere thought of putting together the flux of perceptions from the vision into a coherent and understandable presentation, as had already been attempted, had been overwhelming. Although it was a daunting task, I felt that the only way to unburden myself from the vision's onerous after-effects would be to unload the volume of impressions I received by writing them down and making sense of them, if only for my own understanding and sanity. Many of the impressions eluded me when I attempted to deliberately make sense of them in a rational way. As if mocking the use of reason, these same impressions naturally and fluidly cohered and made a lot of sense when I did not let the act of intellectualizing interfere with the process of my understanding. It was through the process of *allowing* that seemingly unrelated and random thoughts came together to form a complete picture and a sensible concept that could only be grasped intuitively.

It took me a few more years to fully comprehend the hallucinatory vision. Based on my subjective understanding and further interpretation, I came up with the following recapitulation of insights:

There was a strong sense of interconnectedness, or non-separation. As exhibited on a number of occasions, my separate individuality seemed to readily morph or merge with various characters. This resulted in an instantaneous 'state of oneness' with whoever was occupying my thoughts at any given moment. When I communicated with a friend with whom I hadn't spoken in years, it was through a *simultaneous thought exchange*: the very moment one of us 'said' something, a response from the other was simultaneously given. Since there was no time delay in our exchange of thoughts, I had the impression that we had become one and the same entity, and our 'dialogue' was taking place within one mind.

Certain lyrics in a worship song we used to sing as Christian children were implicitly revealed to be literally true: ask, and it shall be given; seek, and you shall find; knock, and the door shall be opened. Not only were these aphorisms exhibited as unexaggerated truths, but there was a consistent impression that there was no time interval between cause and effect – *asking and receiving are simultaneous; seeking and finding happen at the same time; and the moment you knock, the door opens.*

There was the bewildering sensation that it was as if the floodgates to a *reservoir of knowledge* had opened up. With this impression, I gained the knowing that all knowledge is, in fact, available and accessible. Accordingly, I truly felt omniscient, enlightened. There are also no secrets. It is simply impossible for anyone to keep a secret from anyone else because of the inexplicable state of non-separation that was strongly implied. If you could meld with anybody, you would know their innermost secrets, and they would know yours too. However, it was extremely ironic that, although the floodgates of knowledge had been thrown open and I could access whatever information I desired, I failed to get a clue about the most important knowledge I had been seeking: how to climb out of the pit trap and be forever free from the sensation of struggling not to drown.

Another striking impression was that everything appeared to be illusory. I could be old, young, wealthy, impoverished, famous, or infamous – but all of these identities are fleeting and can change in the blink of an eye. In fact, these attributes appear to be nothing more than shifting ideas and thoughts we hold in our minds. And these ideas belong to a realm – the reservoir of knowledge – where an *infinite* number of ideas, or 'information' are found. We could pick any of these ideas from the reservoir and transform them into tangible reality simply by consistently focusing our attention on them.

As regards to time, when I was in that hallucinatory state, what came to me was that there is no 'time' as we know it, but that everything is happening at the same time in a seemingly *one great whirling eternal present moment*. It appears that time is also just an idea – a thought projection created by the mind as it imagines a past, a future, and a present that are distinct and separate from one another. So that when I perceived time to have stood still, it was in fact my thinking mind which momentarily stood still – my mind stopped projecting time. And when I perceived that there was *nothing* (no-thing) in existence, it was simply because I stopped thinking and, as a result, I *stopped projecting*. I had the impression that everything, including time, is created by the act of thinking, and that if the *stream of thoughts* that is continually creating and recreating the world were to cease flowing, the world, or *reality* as we know it, would crash and cease to exist.

Through what we are thinking, believing, and declaring as real, it is *us* – the source of thoughts – who are the sustainers of this whole, illusory reality.

The most unsettling impression of all was the unpleasant sensation of drowning, suffocation, and gasping inside an invisible trap with a pervasive presence. Inside this pit-trap-like realm, it appears that we have the choice, the ability, or the power to be whatever we want to be and to do whatever we want to do. There is, nonetheless, a very disturbing feeling that although we are very powerful beings and are capable of great feats, there appears to be *nothing new* in our reality. Accordingly, everything seemed hollow and meaningless, including our many endeavors, achievements, dramas, and even our angst, strivings, and struggles. And it was intimated that death is not the way out of this cyclical yet static state we are trapped in. This particular impression proved to be the most compelling of all. It left a lingering, hauntingly melancholic residue in my awareness, even long after I had recovered from that bizarre vision.

♥ ♥ ♥

Although I regarded the overall result of my 'vision quest' to be a success, I regarded my experience of "enlightenment" to be a disaster. Mercy was the next person I told my vision story to. Unlike my travel friend, she took me seriously; she did not laugh or doubt my story. Her sympathetic and concerned comment was that I had either gotten sick from food poisoning resulting in a distressing hallucination, or I had been momentarily possessed by an evil spirit-being native to that remote island. I reasoned that perhaps I should have listened to her. I should have stopped asking and dwelling on unholy questions. As the boy from my elementary school had warned me, perhaps I should not have been deliberately visiting wild and remote places – potential hotspots for sorcery. As my former co-worker had admonished, perhaps I should not have been emptying my mind in meditation so as to have prevented the Devil from creeping into my consciousness and distorting my normal perception. Because after my enlightenment, after my eyes were opened to the great emptiness and illusory nature of everything, nothing mattered to me anymore. I lost any motivation to do or desire anything. For what does it matter if I command the whole world if I am confined in a pit trap?

I had presumed that enlightenment would bring bliss, but, to me, it was the opposite of bliss. It was certainly not fun to be awakened to the realization that one is mired in a repetitive cycle in a shadowy pit-trap reality.

36

LIFE AFTER DEATH

It was intimated in my hallucinatory vision that death is not the end. When I heard the words 'on earth as it is in heaven,' the first thing that came to mind was the enigma that had long perplexed Mother: *what you lose on earth, you lose in heaven*. I may have stumbled upon the answer to Mother's riddle.

When I was, presumably, freed from my earthly body, yet did not feel liberated from the trap, I subtly understood that a soul, or the consciousness that leaves a body, does not go to either a heaven or a hell destination. Contrary to the paradisiacal promises illustrated in religious pamphlets peddled by evangelists, the grass is not greener on the other side. Since what I think of as 'me' is only an *idea*, a *mental formation*, a *piece of thought* within consciousness, where I go after I die is equally just an idea colored by my *perception* of where I believe I will go after I die. This explains why, in accounts of near-death experiences, a Christian sees Jesus, a Buddhist sees Buddha, and a pagan sees their ancestors greeting them. So, it appears that who we meet after we die is determined by our belief systems rather than by a single objective standard. This merely demonstrates that no one has a monopoly on truth.

After leaving the earthly plane of matter, a person's soul or consciousness simply slips into a parallel reality – a world or dimension compatible with the reality to which that consciousness is attuned. A person's level of awareness and state of being, as well as their belief system, determine the kind of reality their soul will experience in a life-after-death situation. When an individual's *consciousness* is experiencing heaven on earth, and this is the feeling, idea, or belief held as the soul or consciousness separates from the body, this state of being or awareness is carried over to the 'next' life on the other side. Thus, it is true, the conundrum, *on earth as it is in heaven*.

The traditional belief of my mountain tribes about life after death provides an apt example to illustrate the esoteric saying, on earth as it is in heaven. Prior to the introduction of the concepts of heaven, purgatory, and hell by Christianity, in my people's traditional cosmology, the fate of a departed soul was largely determined by its temperament. It is believed that the souls of the dead join their ancestors in the afterlife. They go into a wide array of places or realms that closely resemble their ways of thinking and doing when they were on earth. It is said that they may continue to engage in the same things and habits they liked to do when they were on earth. For example, someone who loves smoking tobacco or drinking alcohol may continue to do so on the other side. And this is why, in the old tradition, people offered tobacco, native wine or alcohol, or whatever the deceased ancestor enjoyed while living on earth. A fun-loving soul will find himself in a realm where he will be reunited with his fun-loving ancestors. A quarrelsome soul will likewise find himself in a realm with other quarrelsome souls. Someone who loves to gamble, someone who loves to sing and entertain, and someone who is helpful, will also find themselves in parallel, albeit *non-physical*, worlds where they will be able to fulfill or express their desires.

The understanding of a multi-world, or multi-realm, is an inherent part of the Igorot people's cosmology. There are not only the two worlds of heaven and earth, or a heaven and a hell. If the likes of heaven and earth do indeed exist, there is not a thick line of demarcation between these two realms. The world 'over there' (the non-physical realm) is not necessarily better or worse than the one 'here' (the physical earth plane). In fact, the different worlds intertwine, and inter-dimensional interactions happen all the time. The pagan Igorot rarely felt compelled to visit the grave of a departed loved one. This is because it is the spirit of the departed who pays a visit to their living relatives through dreams, spirit possessions, or in the form of animals, or through other traditionally recognized signs. A medium can also summon the spirit of the departed to assist with the 'diagnosis' of an illness that has befallen a living relative.

The bodies of those who die from sudden and violent causes are handled differently from those who die in the usual manner, like illness and old age. Customarily, the former are buried in special sites and positioned in certain positions according to the manner in which death came upon them. Those who die in unexpected and violent circumstances, such as accidents, homicides, or battles, are treated differently because it is believed that their temporal or human consciousness might not have been prepared to transition smoothly, leaving them traumatized or in a state of confusion. To address such incidences, certain shamanic rituals and practices are observed.

Warriors who died in battle were not buried in their ancestral burial grounds because their warrior souls were believed to follow and mimic the living warriors of their clan or tribesmen when they went to battle. Meanwhile, on the other side of the mountain, the victorious party in a battle would be celebrating their victory as well as performing rituals to protect themselves from the vengeful spirit of their fallen opponent and his living relatives.

The death of those who die of natural causes, such as old age, is celebrated rather than mourned. There are those who are said to have lived their lives to the fullest, serving and giving generously to their communities. Their wakes, which can last a week or more, are marked by grand feasts. And the only reason their relatives 'fear' their death is because their journey to another world requires elaborate rituals and costly celebrations.

The preceding examples show how the world of the living is reflected in the world of the dead, and vice versa. If there are battles to be fought here, there are battles to be fought there as well. If you live your life in peace and ease here, you can expect to experience a restful life of ease there as well. And just as there are various realities or dimensions in the world of the living, there are as many dimensions or realms in the world of the dead.

Undoubtedly, the Igorots do not see death as the end of life. Death was not feared in and of itself, since the souls of the departed continued to exist in non-physical realms. Instead, the Igorots were more concerned with how a person died or how a soul transitioned, believing that it was critical to assist and guide a departing soul to ensure a smooth journey and a more pleasant experience on the other side. They believed that the living could actually help the souls of the departed, just as the souls of the departed could be practically tapped to help the living in their earthly lives.

37

ON EARTH, AS IT IS IN HEAVEN

A marked resemblance shared by Christianity and the other religious traditions I came across is the underlying belief in a *future time* – where life is believed to be better than it is *now*. A devotee of the Hindu sect group I hung around with told me that his strict adherence to the austere practices laid down by the tradition of his sect was founded on the belief that all struggles and sufferings in this life were caused by negative karma incurred in a less virtuous or moral previous existence. Their current efforts to strive to live a disciplined and righteous existence in this life will thus guarantee them a better life in a future incarnation. As a Christian, Mother, too, had been yearning for that future time when Satan would be bound and locked in the abyss. That time when Jesus returns and reigns for a Thousand Years with the resurrected righteous people – the Believers – who will finally be able to live better lives because Satan will not be around to mess them up. One could argue that this religious belief, pertaining to a better life in some future time, is no different from the communist atheists' hopes and dreams of a brighter future society, which would presumably ensue from their present-day efforts, struggles, and sacrifices. This common belief among many people, whether Believers or Unbelievers, seems to speak of a collective unconscious belief that self-denial, pain, and allowing hardships and sufferings in the present moment are good and even desirable, as they are the *key* to a better future.

However, if the conundrum on earth, as it is in heaven, has the same meaning as what you lose on earth, you also lose in heaven, then, not unless a soul finds heaven here on earth, heaven above, or heaven in other *future* planes of existence or incarnation, would remain elusive. In the Igorot worldview, there is no notion of a reward or punishment to be gained in the afterlife. As the worlds above and the worlds below, the worlds on the other side and the worlds on this side are non-physical and physical mirrors of each other, there is only the *here and now* moment to live and be happy in. Heaven can be experienced not only in an abstract, non-physical realm but also on earth, with its wondrous material nature teeming with spirits and abundant in resources that sustain and nourish the transitory physical experience.

Human religious culture has strayed very far from the basics by developing multilayered, complex constructs and belief systems in the form of sophisticated doctrines and rigid dogmas that are administered by an institutionalized hierarchy of priests and spiritual leaders, further confusing the already bewildered layperson. In maintaining that it is normal and even beneficial to endure a life of strife and suffering on earth, since happiness and victory over adversity await the Believer in heaven, the masses are shepherded to pine for a better life somewhere else, some other time, so that they are conditioned to tolerate a lesser life on earth and accept it as their normal, unalterable lot.

To their credit, the world's organized religious cultures provide a context in which the masses can grapple with the human condition and make sense of life on earth, despite their labyrinthine and escapist alternative routes. There is undeniably some consolation and relief in the idea that, in the future, a messiah for the religious or an extraterrestrial liberator for the New Ager will descend from above and free humanity from its shackles and fetters. Unfortunately, however, such a storyline is contrary to the fundamental esoteric wisdom: *as above, so below*. The widely established and well-organized strategy of the world's religions for coping with life on Earth has devolved into a well-maintained snare.

38

GLASS BUBBLE WORLDS

About four years after my hallucinatory experience on the island, I had a very similar dream to that of the poignant pit trap impression. In my dream, I saw the entire world in a dimly lit movie theater. The entire world was engrossed in watching a movie. The movie screen resembled a massive computer screen. All eyes and attention were focused on the movie, which was perceived as real by the moviegoers. At one point in the dream, I, too, was inside the movie theater, and I could agree that the movie was very interesting, except that, I noticed, the plot was nothing new. It appeared to be an old story being revived over and over again in different times and locations, with a different set of actors playing the same roles. I was about to make a casual remark about the movie to the man seated to my right when I sensed he did not want to be bothered. He was laughing at what he was seeing in the movie. I turned to the woman to my left, but she too sent the vibe that she did not want to be disturbed. She was crying at what she was seeing in the movie. It amused me that the same scene in a movie could make one person cry and another laugh.

As I watched the people watching the movie, it occurred to me that it was only their *collective perception* that made the movie seem real, because from my vantage point outside the movie theater, they were only looking at a man-made movie! Then I noticed that the movie theater and the people in it were enclosed in what appeared to be a large bubble. I simultaneously became aware of the distraught and world-weary faces of the moviegoers. I thought that, as it was merely a bubble encasing the whole world, it could easily burst and everyone inside would be freed. A closer look revealed, however, that the bubble was thicker than it appeared.

Nobody among the moviegoers seemed to be aware that they were watching a movie in a dark space contained within a glass bubble. I thought, if only somebody would poke at the glass bubble to make noise, the viewers' one-pointed attention on the movie would be momentarily broken, long enough for someone to notice their confinement and inform the others. I had the idea of hurling a stone; even if it did not have enough impact to break the huge thick glass, it might distract some people, so they would notice their confinement. I looked around for a stone, but could not find any. And then, a most astonishing revelation took place: it was the moviegoers' age-old, deep-seated, complex, and tangled thoughts, which, over eons, had consistently woven a membrane that had solidified into an impenetrable, hard glass bubble. I knew then that the bubble could only be cracked from the inside – from its very source. As this almost frightening realization struck me, my body involuntarily convulsed and I awoke from the dream.

The world's prevalent and enduring thoughts compounded, gained density, and formed a spherical aquarium-like glass bubble that confined a whole world which is totally oblivious of its confinement.

The dream aptly reminded me of another dream-vision I had, but had not thoroughly understood until the aforementioned dream shed more light on it:

I was taking a nap in the late afternoon. As I was about to fall asleep, the loud, strained holler of a chicken egg embryo peddler startled me. I grumbled about why the peddler would not just stop taking that uphill route near my house when, as I observed, no one in the neighborhood seemed to be buying chicken egg embryos. I wondered whether his daily hard work selling egg embryos was worth straining and cracking his vocal cords. As these thoughts ran through my sleepy head, I had a spontaneous hypnagogic image of the peddler. I saw his *thoughts* enshrouding his entire body like a cocoon, inadvertently insulating him from a bigger reality or possibility. Visually, his thoughts appeared like a thick mist or fog that sealed him off from the larger world or reality. And with the kinds of thoughts he thought about himself, about other people, and about the world, he created his own personalized glass bubble world.

The hypnagogic image of the peddler implied that his bubble world is formed by what is going on inside his mind. Only he could break his confining glass bubble world from the inside by changing his habitual way of thinking. But since he was unable to stretch, expand, or pierce through his limiting thoughts, he was unable to think beyond selling chicken egg embryos, or at least changing his trade route. He had no awareness that it was the thoughts he thought that were shaping his personal reality. Above all, he was unaware that he possessed the inherent ability to alter the way he thought. As a result, he ended up living his life unconsciously, going through the same motions every day, even if it did not produce a better result. Since there was no departure from his limited way of thinking, there was no innovation in his actions and thus no change in his circumstances.

39

IT IS NOT REAL

Paradoxically, it was my dreaming of the 'glass bubble worlds' while sleeping that jolted me awake from a gloomy and troubling dream I had been unconsciously dreaming while awake! These dreams revealed to me how I had created my own glass bubble world through my thoughts, in which I persistently believed and perceived myself and the world I live in to be doomed to meaningless suffering and repetition. I came to realize that my heavy impression of being trapped in a pit trap was, in effect, only a reflection of my strongly held beliefs about life and reality.

The pit trap, too, is not real. The pit trap world, like everything else created by thought, is not an exemption from being a mere *idea*, and is not exempt from being an *illusory reality*, no matter how deeply affected and convinced I was of its apparent reality. I came to learn that having a strong emotional reaction to certain things and happenings does not necessarily make those things and happenings the ultimate reality – at least not in the experience of everybody. The trap, the confinement, the suffering, existed only in my mind. Although they are only ideas or impressions amongst many other ideas and impressions that simultaneously exist in my consciousness, as I constantly dwelt and believed in the absolute reality of these particularly gloomy ideas, I *activated* them, and then saw them happen around me – within the confines of my bubble world.

Life, as defined, imagined, or lived as suffering, is merely a dream; one of many concurrent dream versions. We can speak of this fact because we know of people who we perceive to be deprived and suffering, but they may not see themselves as deprived or suffering. We have also met people who appear to have everything, yet they believe themselves to be lacking one or more things. Everything in life is relative. Although all of humanity does share a *common hallucination*, for example, the moviegoers who were mesmerized by a movie they believe to be real, it is also a simultaneous fact that in this multi-reality we exist in, each individual has his or her own *separate experiential journey*. Everyone lives in their own bubble world, as demonstrated by the man and woman in the movie theater who responded in contrasting ways to exactly the same scene in the movie.

The chicken egg embryo peddler, whom I deemed to be living a substandard existence, had taught me an invaluable metaphysical lesson: he made me aware that I, too, had created my own limiting glass bubble world – that of gloom and doom. Since I was totally unconscious that I had been dreaming my life to be some gloom-and-doom reality, I had again been crying and lamenting over a mere *dream*!

40

THE WAY OUT OF THE TRAP

I realized that I had been caught in a *cycle of cause and effect*, or karma. I had steeped myself in the feeling of being trapped, or existing in a fettered reality. The effect of this perception on me was that it made the idea of a fettered reality come alive and manifest in my personal world. *The effect* – the materialization of this somber idea in the world around me – further reinforced and fortified *the cause* – my already existing belief in the truth and validity of a limited reality.

It is logical, then, that the way out of the trap is to stop dwelling on ideas of limitation, sorrow, strife, and suffering, lest these thought-forms magnify, vivify, and then congeal into tangible reality. Instead, in order to break the age-old, limiting habitual ways of thinking that resulted in a crystallized glass bubble enclosure, a new, different cause must be launched in order to manifest a new, desired effect.

In a multi-world reality where freedom to choose – freedom to perceive, freedom to interpret, and freedom to imagine – is a birthright, anyone is capable of choosing whether to live in a gloomy, depressed world or in a bright, delightful world. Every individual creates his or her own reality as each individual focuses on ideas and beliefs that either depress or uplift. One can play the role of the rich or the poor, the beautiful or the ugly, the aggressor or the victim. In this *dream world*, there is no limit to the possibilities a person can imagine and experience. One can be trapped in a dreary cyclical reality, reincarnating over and over again, or one can choose to break free and transcend the cycle by simply unsubscribing from the broadcast, or belief system, that is maintaining that reality.

Contrary to the popular belief held by those who are urging us to leave the material earth and ascend to the kingdom of God above, or by those who teach that having a physical body is a punishment, the so-called carnal sinful body is not a trap. Punishing and depriving the body of its needs is not what brings spiritual liberation, nor will it bring the end of suffering. This is because, even if one escapes the confines of the body through death or an out-of-body experience, one may still feel trapped if the trap is heavily *imprinted* on one's consciousness. The trap, hell, heaven, and happiness are all states of consciousness. *And one's state of consciousness is what determines one's experiences in life, as well as in the afterlife.*

In the eternal continuum of existence, physical death does not bring the end. Death does not erase, nullify, or invalidate anything that ever existed or will ever exist. But when a soul finally realizes that there is no sinful past and no future redemption, liberation happens in the here and now. Karma is then canceled, and the wheels of reincarnation come to a halt.

41

THE WILL OF MAN

Grandma and I were out in the yard, as usual, sunning ourselves. I was probably around seven years old at the time because, as I recall, I had just started going to school.

We were distracted by a puppy's loud cries. The puppies were fighting each other. The black puppy had the white puppy pinned down. Blackie clamped and pulled Whitey's ear with its tiny canine teeth. As if that wasn't enough, as Whitey tried to flee, the excitedly growling and jumping Blackie grabbed the fallen puppy's hind leg, and with all its might, it dragged away the shrieking Whitey. The cruel commotion did not seem to bother the mother dog, who watched them detachedly. In an attempt to rescue Whitey from its pitiful predicament, I hurled my slipper at the aggressive puppy.

"What are you doing?" Grandma asked.

"They are fighting. I'm *saving* Whitey," I said, matter-of-factly.

Grandma chuckled and assured me that the puppies were only having fun. I insisted that Blackie was trying to kill Whitey, causing the latter to cry out in agony, which is obviously not fun for the underdog.

"Blackie is not going to kill its brother. As I and their mother see it, they are only playing an exciting puppy game," Grandma said, indicating the mother dog with a small movement of her chin.

I looked at the mother dog. She just sat there with total composure, unaffected, lovingly watching her puppies. She also looked at me, and the gentle look in her eyes seemed to confirm

Grandma's opinion that the puppies were just playing.

As she watched her puppies wrestle, the mother dog was very tolerant, allowing, and unconditional. I was very upset by the mother dog's non-action, so I attempted to rescue Whitey and punish Blackie, but Grandma calmed me down by assuring me that all was well, and it was all just a game.

Like the wise and loving dog, God, too, permits everything. I couldn't fathom God's mind, why He created Lucifer and allowed evil and suffering to exist in this world. It is now my understanding that what God gave man was not the freedom to sin, but the freedom to experience and explore everything man can conceive and imagine in his mind.

With absolute freedom bestowed upon man, we can therefore conclude that the Will of God automatically upholds the will of man. To put it simply, man's will is God's Will, and vice versa. So, if the Will of God yields to the will of man, contrary to the stories told, God is not, after all, a controlling, manipulative, possessive, and punitive God. God is an allowing God.

The fact that man was given the freedom to shape his own reality clearly indicates that man is *fully empowered* by God. In his freedom and ability to conceive ideas, to focus and mold things into existence, man, not God nor the Devil, is fully responsible for the kind of world he creates. Through the quality of his thoughts, the caliber of the ideas he upholds, and according to the bounds of his imagination, man is free to create a world of splendor, or a world of squalor.

And yet, in the grand scheme of things, to the boundless, all-encompassing, unconditional, infinite, and allowing God, whatever man chooses to create and experience – *none of it matters* – for wherever man is, whatever his position is in the illimitable multi-world – along the inexhaustible spectrum of life experiences he may choose to experience – however he may choose to journey through the darkest, bottomless pits of the infernal worlds, or through the ecstatic heights of the heavenly states of enlightenment – none of these will change a thing in man's basic, original nature. For in the end, after all that has been said and done between God and Satan, after all the elaborate play of light and dark, whatever each individual human has gone through, the mortal one, eventually, will *Awaken*, to find himself nowhere else but at *Home* – dreaming, ironically, that he is somewhere else, doing something else, and being someone else.

If, somewhere along the eternal flow of his dreaming, man experiences a particularly unpleasant journey, he will be relieved upon awakening to realize that it was all just a dream. Upon *Awakening*, he will find himself unimpaired, undiminished, complete, and totally safe. If he has a pleasant journey, the moments of it will forever delight his soul. Then, using his God-given free will, he can *will* himself back to sleep and dream yet another dream – for it is the thrill of the experience, the fun of the journey, that is constantly summoning the *primordial creator* within him to embark on yet another adventure, which he discovers is, after all, worth all the trouble of experiencing life on earth.

We *dream* and *create* multi-reality projections, but we never leave heaven – our Home. We dream and create a gap between ourselves and the Creator, but we have never been separated from the Creator – our True Selves.

42

ONLY A STORYTELLING

Without a formidable opposition, there would be no great hero. Without the Devil, there would be no reason for God to exist – and vice versa. In the Bible story of Job, we are not the helpless little pawns caught in the crossfire of God and Satan's game. But it is actually us, in our powerful virtual reality games, who are pitting, cheering, and exhorting our imagined champion, God, against our imagined adversary, Satan. We enjoy dramatic stories because they are exciting, and, as Apu once said, life, or energy flow, thrives on excitement.

The concepts of impurity and purity, sinner and saint, sin and redemption, suffering and liberation, karma and reincarnation, are all labels used to describe certain conditions or states of consciousness that are based on man's subjective perception of his experiences. The rivalry between Believer and Unbeliever, The Great Battle Between Good and Evil, The Fall of Man, The Lake of Fire, The Original Sin: all of these stories are told to describe man's epic dream journey. They are both real and not real at the same time. They are real because man's feelings and experiences are real, but they are also not real because, like everything else that exists besides *Consciousness*, they are illusory. They are a product of the creative imaginations of storytellers who have a penchant for using vivid words and evocative constructs to make a story more entertaining to tell.

Similarly, the stories told in this book are only a description of one person's experiences, inspired by her dreams and hallucinations. They are both real and not real.

43

THE GREAT STORYTELLER

The Great Storyteller is the narrator of all tales, the describer of all descriptions, the definer of all definitions, the one who conceives ideas, the one who paints pictures in all colors, the one who sings songs in all tunes, and the one who declares what is real, and what is not real.

The Great Storyteller is like the ever-flowing ugwor in the forest – the source of infinite ideas, creatively spun and woven into intricate designs and colorful images – springing to life – forming multi-realities in multi-worlds.

The Great Storyteller is the Ultimate Dreamer – the conjurer of both pagan magic and religious miracles.

Finally, the Great Storyteller automatically favors the will of man, for *within* man dwells the Great Storyteller.

44

CLOSING RIDDLE

If I am a temporary storyteller relating equally temporary stories, what is the purpose of my temporary act of relating these equally temporary stories?

EPILOGUE

I take occasional trips to my hometown. The last time I was there, I went walking around the neighborhoods. I could not help but notice how unusually quiet and deserted the neighborhoods had become. Although silence is actually the norm because by mid-morning, everyone who is fit to work will have already gone to their workplaces, I had the feeling that something was missing. I recalled that when I was little, it was a common sight to see grandparents and their grandchildren playing, sunning, or telling stories in the open yards of their homes. But these days, the yards are totally deserted. The doors and windows of houses are shut. The only sign of life, the indication that the houses are not abandoned by their owners, is the presence of dogs, chickens, and pigs. As I strolled, observing the changes, I thought that it seems, nowadays, people do not live very long like Grandma did. There are no more old people, the grandparent mentors of the young ones. Or perhaps the community no longer needs these grandparent mentors, and that is why the elders choose to exit much earlier than they used to. Indeed, the new system in place is that while parents are at work, children, even the very young ones, are deposited inside classrooms to be 'educated' according to a prescribed curriculum that must be adhered to. Each village now operates a daycare center for preschoolers, and the public elementary school has added two levels of kindergarten to accommodate five-and six-year-olds.

On the way back to my house, I passed by a relative's now uninhabited house. I remembered my cousin and how we used to play in their open yard under the watchful gaze of his grandmother. His own apu had also told him countless stories, which he committed to memory right up to this day. I have very good reasons to believe that he does remember them all, and vividly well, even more than I remember the stories passed on to me by my apu. Because although my cousin is not very fond of talking, all that I am unable to express in words and in writing, he is able to eloquently express in his oil paintings that are in demand in many parts of the world. If one of these days, you happen to behold one of his masterful paintings, you will acquire a silent understanding of the reality of the unusual events, the inter-dimensional affairs, and the fantastic stories that I have partly, yet dimly, attempted to relate through the pages of this book. They are stories that have occurred, and perhaps still occur, in that dreamy, faraway little hometown.

ABOUT THE AUTHOR

The author is a member of an indigenous group collectively known as the Igorots. The Igorots occupy the mountain ranges of north-central Luzon, the Philippines. For more than three hundred years of the Spanish Empire's occupation of the Philippines, the Igorots were able to defy the attempts of the Spanish Empire to turn them into Christian converts and tribute-paying subjects to the King of Spain. This event allowed the continuation of Igorot indigenous beliefs and ways of life, but earned them the notoriety of being primitive pagan enemies of God and the State. After the conquistadors left, an antagonistic colonial legacy endured between the mountain-dwelling Igorots and the colonized, Christianized, and "civilized" lowland Filipino population.

The Spanish conquistadors were said to have offended the Igorot warriors so much that when the American colonizers adopted a soft strategy policy in dealing with the mountain tribes, such as paying for labor rather than forcing the Igorots to do work for the Americans, the stark contrast to the Spaniards' brutal manners made the Americans look good in comparison. As a result, the Igorots fell into the American colonial fold without resistance. Notwithstanding the Americans' success in taming the Igorots and, although they are now mostly integrated and Christianized, compared to the majority of the Filipino people, the Igorots are still able to maintain their age-old customs and traditions.

The Igorot culture and traditional way of life are founded on animism. Spirit beings are acknowledged to abound everywhere, and they interact with human beings. As in any animistic society, indigenous priests and priestesses exist as intermediaries between the physical world and the spirit world. To a varying degree of ability and sensitivity, before the full-blown entry of external factors such as religion, the public school system, and other modern influences, any adult Igorot inherently understood the natural and contextual codes of his world and, thus, could directly communicate with the invisible realms which are very much a part of his normal world. However, when it comes to the ability to heal illnesses, there are those whose knowledge and abilities are evidently greater than the general populace. These individuals earned the reputation of being *monsop-ok*, or shamans. These healers, mediums, diviners, dreamers, and visionaries, are sought by people when they are ill, whether it be physically, emotionally, mentally, or psychologically. Shamanizing is usually an inherited practice, as the ability is believed to run in families that carry such a particular propensity. Among the author's particular ethnic group, most shamans are women, although men-shamans are not unheard of.

It is of this shamanic lineage that the author claims to have descended from. From both of her parents' clans lived generations of powerful shamans. The author, however, was only able to personally interact with her maternal grandmother, who was the last shaman of her kind in her hometown when she died. It is from this background and context that the author found inspiration to write a philosophical discourse through an indigenous, but contemporary Igorot individual's perspective.

In addition to the author's claim of cultural qualification for writing a culture-based narrative, she is formally educated with a Bachelor of Arts degree in the Social Sciences and a Master of Arts degree in International Relations.

Made in the USA
Las Vegas, NV
13 August 2023